Lectures on Core Microeconomics

LECTURES ON CORE MICROECONOMICS

BHARAT R. HAZARI
AND
CHEUK-YIN HO

Nova Science Publishers, Inc.
New York

For permission to use material from this book please contact us:
Telephone 631-231-7269; Fax 631-231-8175
Web Site: http://www.novapublishers.com

Library of Congress Cataloging-in-Publication Data

Hazari, Bharat R.
Lectures on core microeconomics / Bharat R. Hazari, Cheuk-Yin Ho.
p. cm.
Lectures delivered at the City University of Hong Kong in the fall semester of 2005-2007.
ISBN 978-1-60692-293-4 (softcover)
1. Microeconomics. I. Ho, Cheuk-Yin. II. Title.
HB172.H395 2009
338.5--dc22
2008041723

Published by Nova Science Publishers, Inc. New York

CONTENTS

PREFACE

These notes are based on the microeconomics lectures delivered in the Master of Science in Applied Economics (MSAE) programme at the City University of Hong Kong. They have been delivered in the fall Semesters of 2005— 2007. The lectures are delivered over a period of thirteen weeks (three hours per week). One should always remember the time constraint involved in delivering lectures. Everything can not be covered; therefore one has to be selective in what is taught. This is the reason for calling these lectures core microeconomics. The topics selected and taught reflect our perceptions and value judgment about core topics in microeconomics. Also the students in this class at the City University of Hong Kong come from a very heterogeneous background which varies a lot; medicine, law, mathematics, engineering, physics, biology, and of course economics. The course is designed teach all these heterogeneous students important topics in microeconomics in a span of thirteen weeks. This is a tough task and many of these students are very ambitious and desirous of doing graduate studies in Europe, Canada, and the US. The feedback on this course has been extremely good from students who are pursuing graduate studies in Britain and the US.

These are lecture notes are neither complete and/or comprehensive. They are written in teaching style. They also vary in level at which different topics are taught and also the depth at which these topics are covered. They should not be taken as a substitute for a textbook but as an aid for reading other textbooks. The feedback on this course has been marvelous and it is this feedback which encouraged us to put these notes in print.

We are grateful to Shuang Yao for contributing to Chapter 7. We thank many students in the MASE programme and Professor Mohan Agarwal for very useful and valuable comments. We also thank Emma McPhee and Yingwen Guo for excellent assistance in preparing the manuscript. The responsibilities for all errors rest with the authors.

Bharat R. Hazari
C.Y.Ho

Department of Economics and Finance
City University of Hong Kong

Chapter 1

CONSUMPTION THEORY

David Kreps (1990) correctly remarked that "The central figure in microeconomic theory is the consumer, and the first step is almost always to provide a model of consumer's behaviour", page (15). We also subscribe to this view; our analysis begins with the theory of consumer behaviour. All of us are consumers but all of us need not be producers. From birth to death we consume goods and services-at birth we begin by consuming milk and at death we require funeral services. It is a whole life of consumption. Economists attempt to provide logical and rational foundations for analyzing the behaviour of a consumer. The theory of utility maximization provides an approach for analyzing the behavior of economic agents and in particular, consumers.[1]

We begin our analysis with the concept of a consumption space. Two words have been used here: consumption and space. We all know the meaning of the former but the latter needs to be defined. The term space has a range of definitions:

- Space is that it is part of the fundamental structure of the universe: a set of dimension in which objects are separated and located, have size and shape.
- Space is part of a fundamental abstract mathematical conceptual framework within which we compare and quantify the distance between objects, their sizes and their shapes and so on.

So what is the space for playing chess: a chess board with 64 squares (black and white). Space for soccer: soccer field. On these spaces we define rules of operation to obtain a meaningful set of results.

For the consumer we define a consumption space denoted by X. This space must have a structure. The space should not be chaotic as we want to establish some sort of order in this space. So let us begin by thinking about dimensionality.

RESTRICTIONS ON CONSUMPTION SPACE X

R 1: X is the non-negative orthant in space n i.e., space of n dimensions or R_+^n. Therefore in R_+^2 it consists of the non-negative orthant of the two-dimensional space.

The dimensionality of the consumption space equals the number of commodities we are analyzing so two dimensional space means that we are dealing with two commodities. To generate some sort of an order in the consumption space X, we always place restrictions. We now provide a few examples.

(a) One-dimensional space:

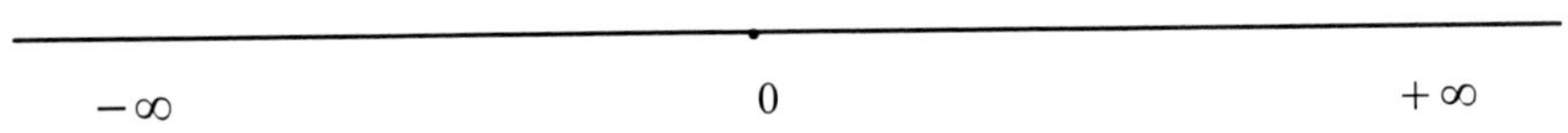

Figure 1.1

Only one good can be represented in this space – it is the real line which goes from $-\infty$ to $+\infty$.

For all illustration purposes we shall use the two-dimensional space.

We now impose restrictions on the consumption space X. The two dimensional space is shown in Figure 1.2.

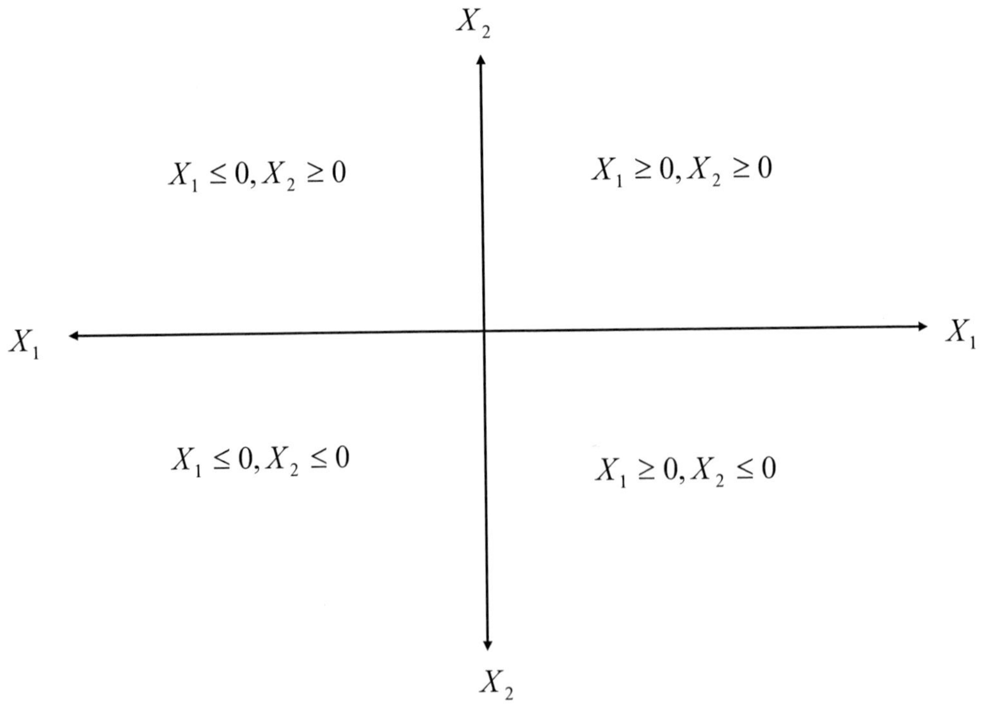

Figure 1.2. Note that the axes belong to more than one quadrant.

Example 1:

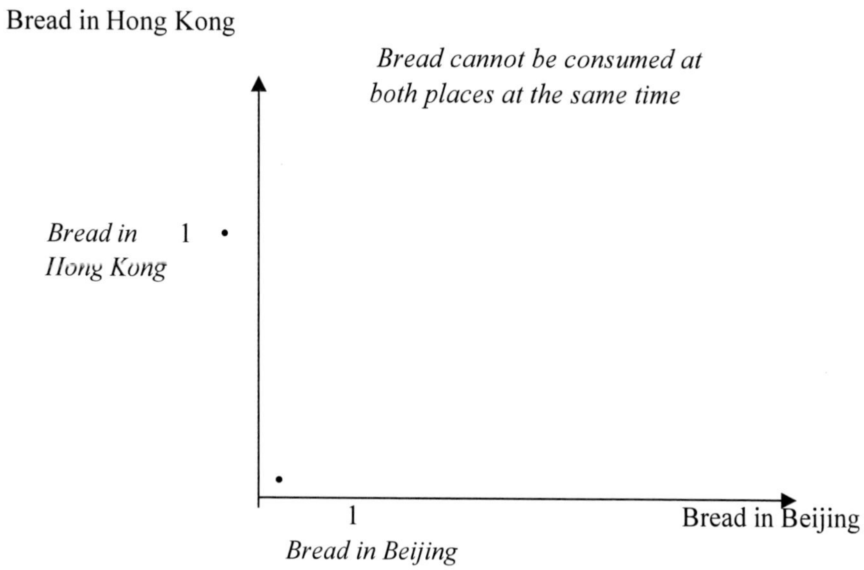

Figure 1.3

Indivisibility: Half a car cannot be purchased

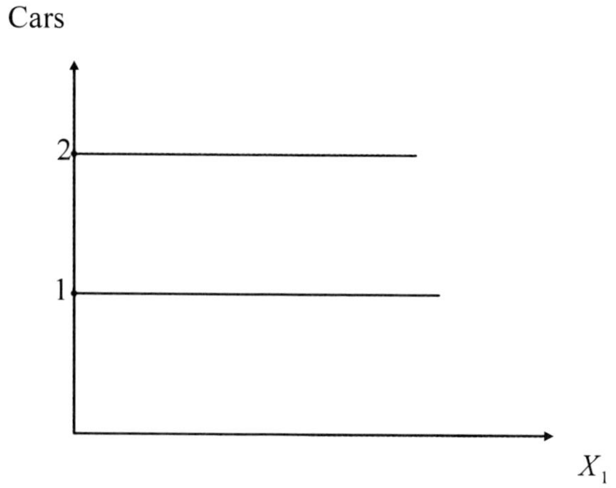

Figure 1.4

Given these examples as illustration of restrictions, we are now going to impose restrictions that are given below.

Definition: Set: A set is a collection of elements.

For example a collection of integers is a set of all integers.

R2: It is assumed that the consumption set is closed and convex.

Definition of closed set: If a set S contains all its boundary points then it is called a closed set.

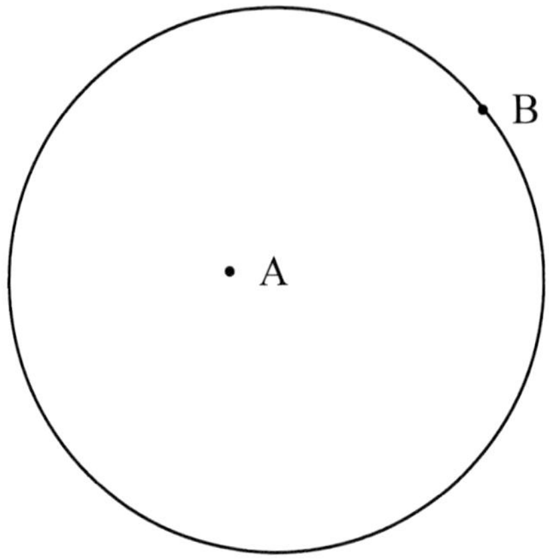

A is an interior point,
B is a boundary point.

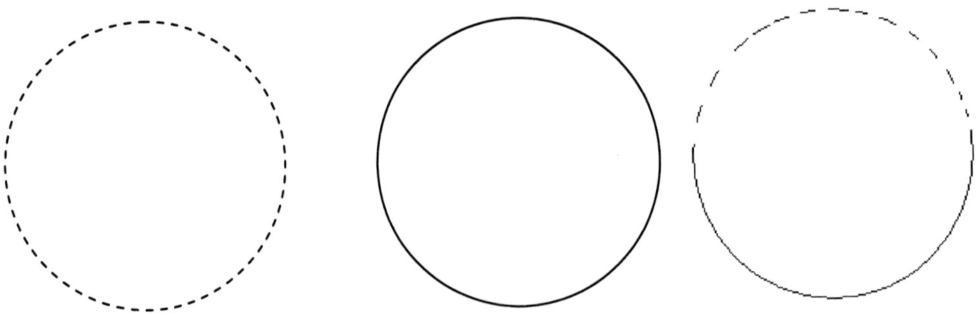

OPEN CLOSED NEITHER OPEN NOR CLOSED

Let us revert back to the non-negative orthant of the two dimensional space. Note that the boundary of this orthant are the horizontal and vertical axes OX_1 and OX_2. These must belong to the set. The set is bounded from below. Subsequently we will place a bound on the consumption set from above.

We now proceed to define convexity. In order to do this we first provide a definition of a linear (convex) combination. Consider two points, X_1 and X_2, let θ take values in the closed interval [0,1]. Then a linear combination is defined as:

$$z = \theta X_1 + (1-\theta)X_2$$

Example: consider $X_1 = 2$ and $X_2 = 6$. Then,

$$4 \quad = \quad (0.5)(2)+(0.5)(6), \text{ where } \theta = 0.5$$

$$2 = (1)(2)+(0)(6), \text{ where } \theta = 1$$

$$6 = (0)(2)+(1)(6), \text{ where } \theta = 0$$

Hence, by varying θ, we can define the entire set of points that are between 2 and 6 including the end points. The end points are joined by a straight line.

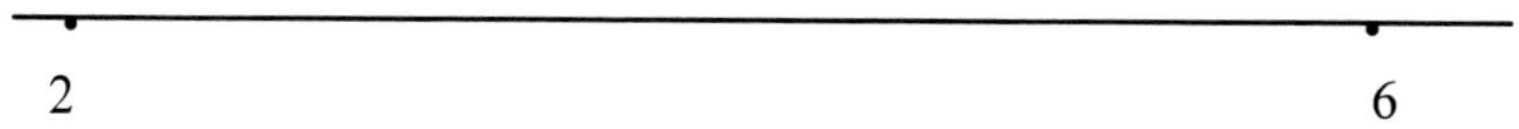

The value of θ between 0 and 1 generates this entire line.

Definition of a convex set: A set S is called convex (strictly convex) if each pair of points in S can be joined by a line segment or a linear combination which belongs to S (interior of S).

Illustration

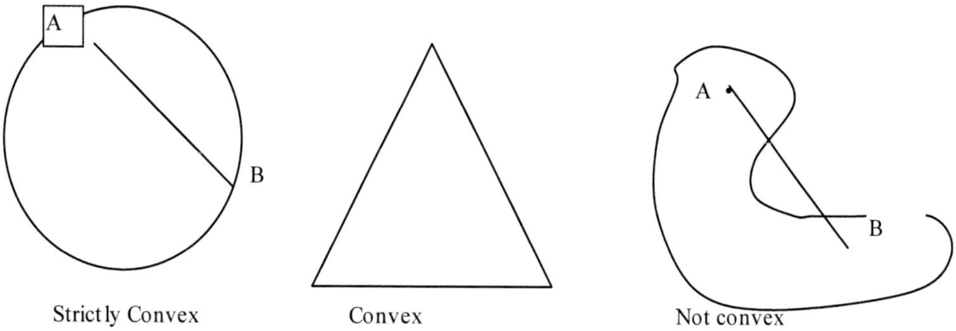

Note that the non-negative orthant of the two-dimensional space is a convex set.

We shall also assume that this space is Euclidean, which implies that it uses a distance function of the following form:

$$distance = d(X_i, Y_i) = \Sigma\left[\left|X_i - Y_i\right|^2\right]^{1/2}$$

We now proceed to define an ordering on the consumption bundles that belong to the consumption space. This ordering will be binary. A binary ordering concerns itself with two elements of the points that belong to any space.

Examples of binary ordering are:

- Taller than
- Fatter than
- Equal to
- Greater than

- Better than or equal to
- Brother of
- and so on.

In the consumption space, we have an infinite number of points. In the two-dimensional space these points consist of bundles of goods as shown in Figure 1.5.

The first number belongs to the horizontal axis and the second to the vertical axis. We shall follow this convention throughout the book. We wish to define consumer preferences on these bundles. This is achieved by introducing the concept of ordering. Let R denote the relation as good as. Let us now define xRy. This means that bundle x is as good as y.

Example:

Let $x = (2,1) =$ consumption bundle consists of 2 units of good 1 and 1 unit of good 2

and $y = (1,2)$

then $(2,1)\ R\ (1,2)$

reads: bundle x (2,1) is as good as bundle y (1,2).

The first property we shall impose on the ordering is completeness.

P 1 Completeness: For all bundles x and y that belong to the consumption space X, either xRy or yRx or both.[2]

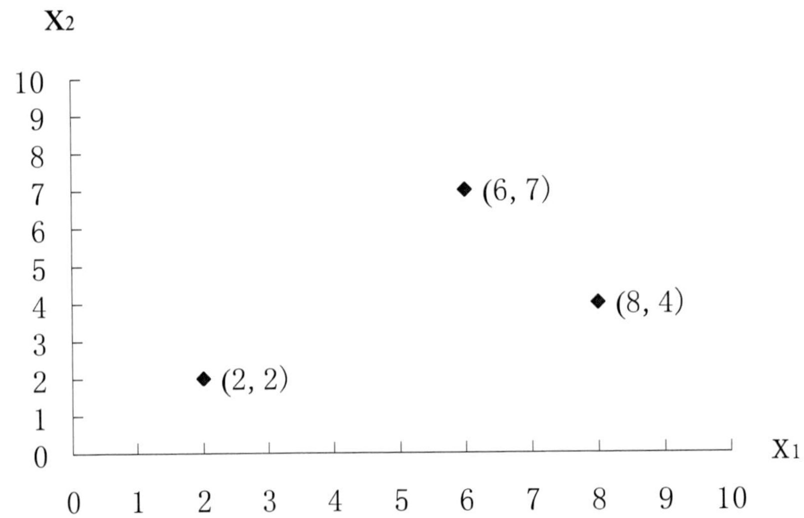

Figure 1.5

P 2 Transitivity: For all bundles x, y and z that belong to the consumption space X, if xRy and yRz, then xRz.

Transitivity is an extremely important property for economic agents. It represents rationality and a large part of economic theory would not survive without this property.

Sports provide good and intuitive example of the violation of transitivity.

Cricket:

Australia defeats South Africa.

South Africa defeats India.

Therefore by transitivity Australia should defeat India. However, India defeats Australia. Hence, can not be defined best. Condocert paradox of voting also provides an example of intransitivity.

By using the concept of ordering both indifference and preference relations can be defined.

Indifference: xRy and yRx together imply that xIy.

Preference: xRy and $\sim yRx$ together imply that xPy. The symbol ~ stands for not. This reads: bundle x is as good as y and bundle y is not as good as x together imply that bundle x is preferred to y.

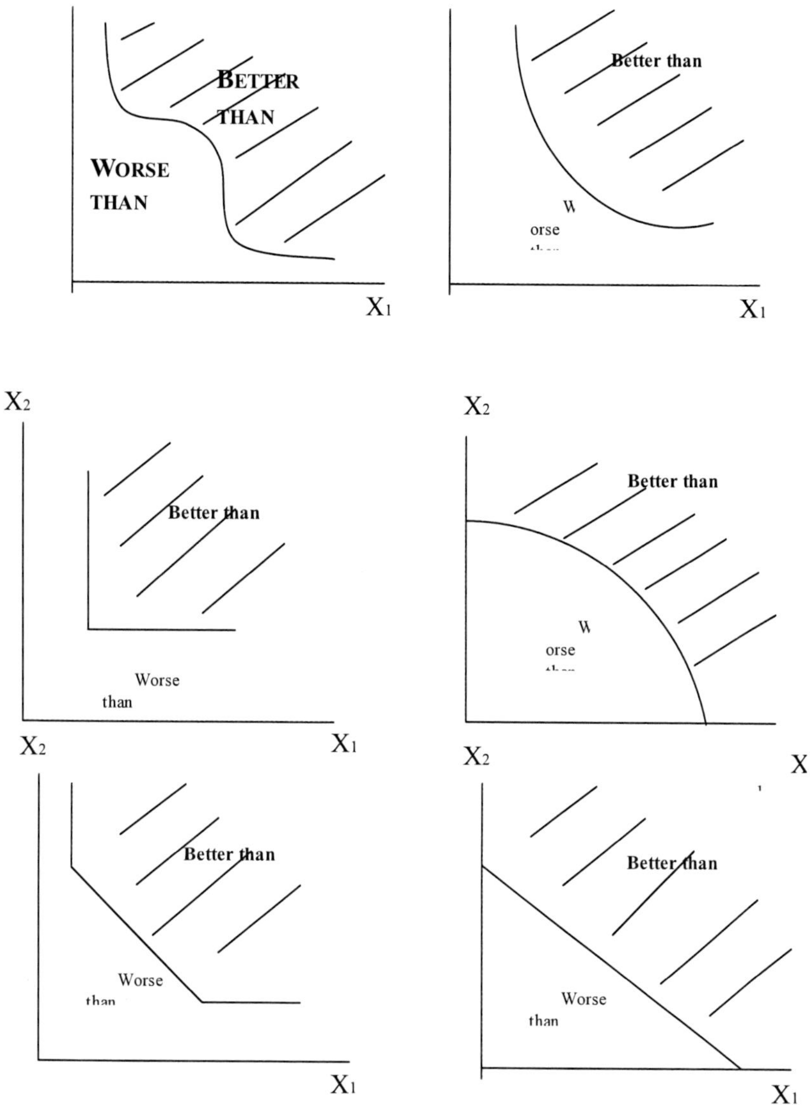

Figure 1.6

We now provide illustration of the use of the concept of indifference. We shall utilize two-dimensional space to achieve this purpose. Consider the following graphs where the points on the line or curve represents all bundles that yield the same satisfaction or all bundles that are equivalent to each other (this curve is known as an indifference curve).

In Figure 1.6 the non-negative orthant is divided into two spaces: the better than space and worse than space. Later on we shall rule out some of these shapes for indifference curves.

Before the publication of the work of Nobel laureate Debreu, it used to be asserted that an ordering that satisfies completeness, reflexivity and transitivity leads to the existence of a utility function. Debreu proved that an additional assumption is required for guaranteeing the existence of a utility function. This axiom is known as continuity. It is better to give examples of orderings that do not satisfy continuity before formally defining it. Consider a lexicographic ordering. All of you at one stage or another have used an object that satisfies the conditions for a lexicographic ordering. The words in a dictionary are lexicographically ordered. Consider the following words: Rat, Cat, At, Bat. How do we order them? We order them in the following manner:

At
Bat
Cat
Rat

What is the nature of this ordering? We order by the first element, then by second and so on. Now consider an example in two-dimensional space. Consider the case of a dipsomaniac. A dipsomaniac always orders his bundles with alcohol first. Consider the following graph where we represent wine on the horizontal and cheese on the vertical axis.

In Figure 1.7 note that *B* is preferred to *A* as it has more wine than *A* but no cheese. It is important to note that no indifference curve can be drawn for this case as there are no points that are indifferent to each other. Can we obtain a utility function for this case? The answer is no and we will come back to discuss this issue.

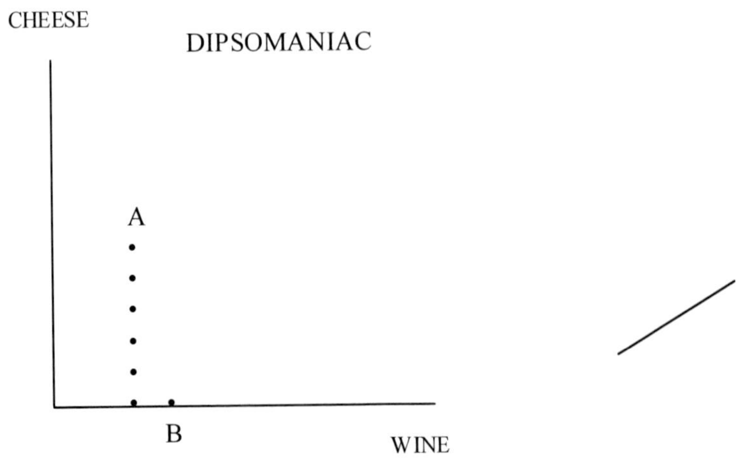

Figure 1.7

Let us now define continuity so that lexicographic orderings can be ruled out.

R3. Continuity: For all bundles y that belong to the consumption space X the set $[x: xRy]$ (better or good as y set) is a closed set and $[y: yRx]$ is also a closed set.

Let us try to explain this. Let us suppose that some bundle y is strictly preferred to z. Note that y is strictly preferred to z. Now consider a bundle which is close enough to y.

Let this bundle be x. Then x must be preferred to z. However, in the case of lexicographic ordering this need not be the case.

Given R1 to R3, we can construct a utility function.

Utility function: Suppose that the ordering R on X is continuous then there exists a continuous utility function $U(X)$ that represents the ordering. For $U(x)>U(y)$, then the consumer strictly prefers bundle x to bundle y. $(U(x) > U(y) \leftrightarrow xPy)$

In microeconomic models in general there are usually a set of n commodities. Given the consumption set R_+^n and each bundle $X \in R_+^n$, (a vector containing the amounts of each commodity) then the utility function maps from $R_+^n \rightarrow R$. Consider the two-dimensional space and let us define an indifference curve in the two dimensional space. The utility function is ordinal and increasing monotonic transformation of this are also utility functions.

Indifference curve: Consists of all bundles that give rise to same level of utility. At this stage we have not imposed sufficient restrictions to generate typical indifference curves which are usually drawn in text books. Consider the following.

Each indifference curve maps into one point on the nonnegative part of the real line. It provides information about the consumers' preferences in an extremely compact manner.

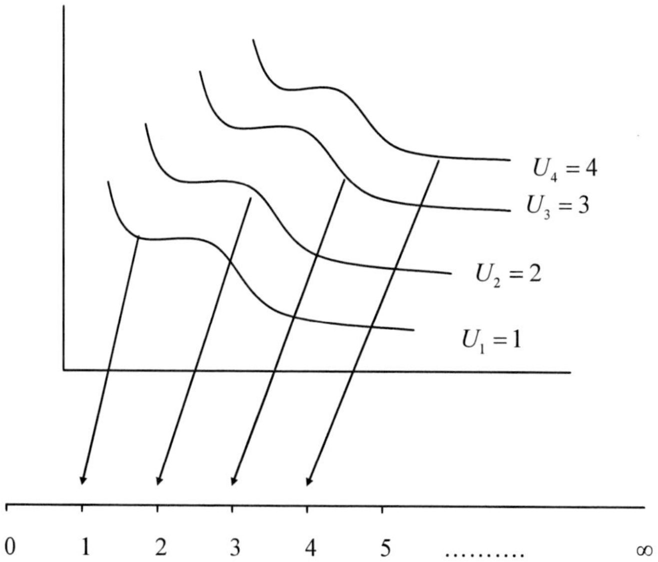

Figure 1.8

Note that this function is ordinal and not cardinal. Hence, any increasing monotonic transformation of the utility function also serves the same purpose.

We now add a few more restrictions on the behavior of the consumer. We now capture the idea that more is preferred to less. For this propose, we introduce two ways of capturing this idea.

Strong monotonicity: If bundle $x \geq y$ and $x \neq y$, then xPy.

Local nonsatiation: Given any bundle x that belongs to the consumption space X and any $\varepsilon > 0$, then there exists some bundle $y \in X$, $|x - y| < \varepsilon$, such that $y\,P\,x$.

Comment 1: meaning of $|x - y|$ in two dimensional space. So x in X has two components and so does y. Hence:

$$\left[(x_1 - y_1)^2 + (x_2 - y_2)^2\right]^{1/2} < \varepsilon$$

Which is nothing other than a circle of the size less than ε.

We discuss these ideas with the help of a graph in the two dimensional space.

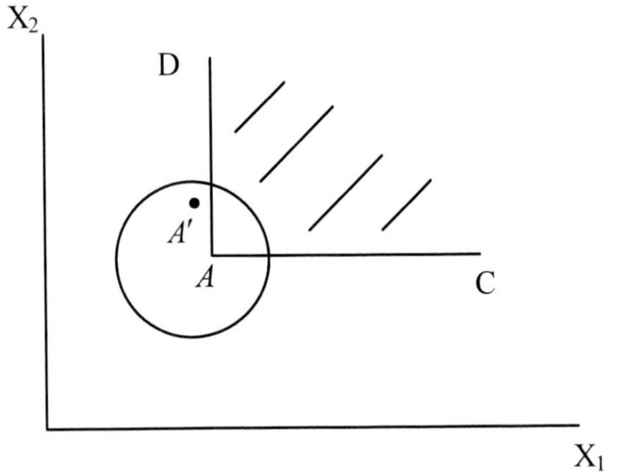

Figure 1.9

Consider the bundle represented by point A. All points on the line AC have more of X_1 but same quantity of X_2, by monotonicity they are preferred to A. Similar logic applies to the segment AD. Now all points in the hatched region have more of both X_1 and X_2, therefore, by monotonicity they are preferred to A. However, monotonicity fails to rank bundles like point A', which belong to the circle drawn around A. This can be ranked by the assumption of local non-satiation, which says that in this circle there exists at least one point that is better than A. Notice that this allows for trade offs between X_1 and X_2 a feature captured by the degree of substitution between X_1 and X_2.

Finally we require two more assumptions to generate a well behaved preference map. All these assumptions are required to ensure that the demand functions have nice properties.

Convexity: Let us consider three bundles x, y and z that belong to the consumption space X. Let us suppose that $x\,I\,z$ and $y\,I\,z$ then convexity implies that for all bundles that belongs to the closed interval [0, 1] the bundle $\lambda x + (1-\lambda)yIz$.

Strict convexity: For $\lambda \in [0,1]$ and $x \neq y$ then $\lambda x + (1-\lambda)yPz$.

The following diagrams illustrate the two types of convexity.

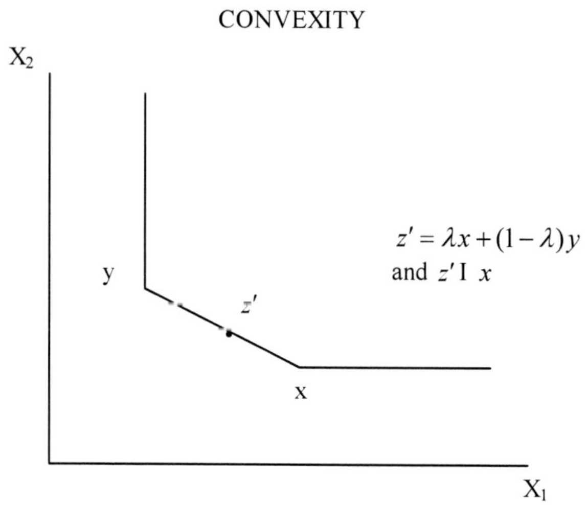

Figure 1.10a

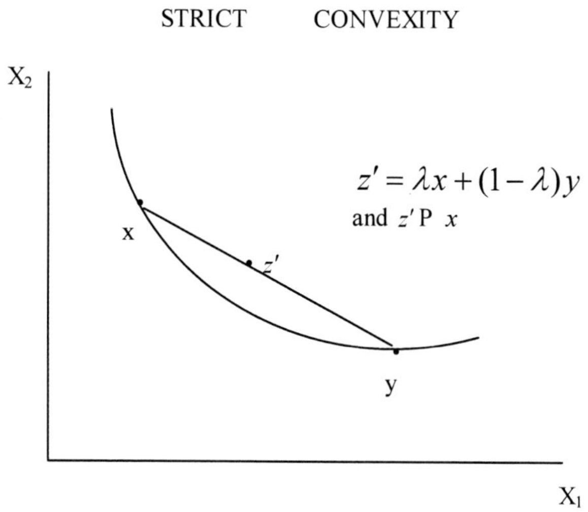

Figure 1.10b

Marginal rate of substitution. This shows us trade offs between different bundles such that the consumer remains on the same level of welfare, that is, on the same indifference curve. We show that:

$$U\lfloor X_1, X_2, ..., X_i, ..., X_j, ...X_n \rfloor$$

This is the n dimensional utility function. For the individual on the same indifference surface we require that:

$$\frac{\partial U}{\partial X_i}dX_i + \frac{\partial U}{\partial X_j}dX_j = 0$$

$$\therefore \frac{dX_j}{dX_i} = -\frac{\partial U / \partial X_i}{\partial U / \partial X_j}$$

This shows the rate at which one good can be substituted for the other. This rate is very important as it shows the arbitrage possibilities between goods. Later we shall introduce a budget constraint which will show the possibilities of arbitrage in the market. Figure 1.11 shows the marginal rate of substitution at different points e, e_1 and e_2. It is important to note that the marginal rate of substitution depends on preferences and the utility function and is independent of the market and prices. The slopes of the line AB, $A'B'$ and $A''B''$ show the marginal rate of substitution at points e, e_1 and e_2 respectively.

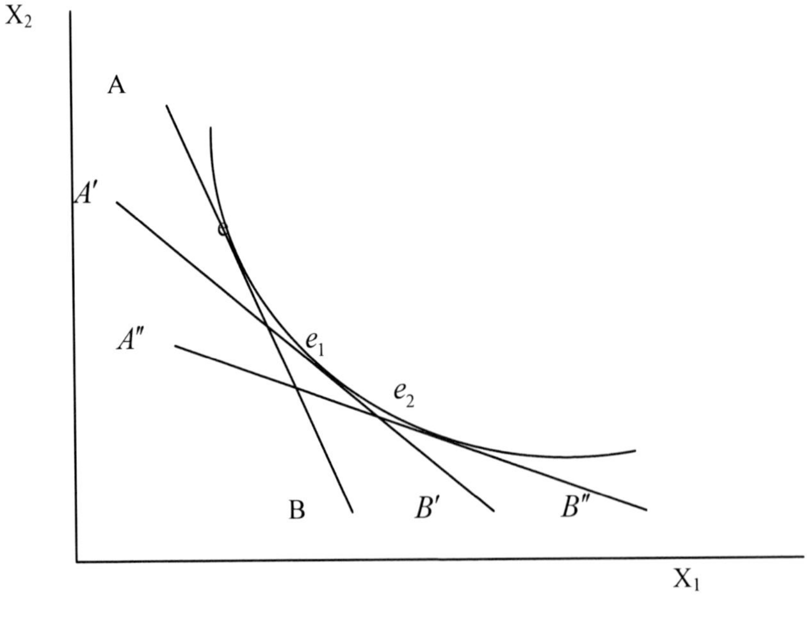

Figure 1.11

It is time to introduce a budget set and a budget constraint. Let there be n goods, hence, the goods vector is $[X_1, X_2, ..., X_n]$. Let us assume that there are n prices $[p_1, p_2, ..., p_n]$ and all these prices are assumed to be positive, that is, $p_i > 0$ for $(i = 1...n)$. We can then form the dot product.

$$p \cdot x = p_1 \cdot X_1 + p_2 \cdot X_2 + p_3 \cdot X_3 + \ldots + p_n \cdot X_n$$

Further we shall assume that **nominal income** *I* and the commodity prices are given from outside. So we have the following information given to us exogenously: nominal income *I*, prices $p_1 \ldots p_n$ and the utility function *U*. We can now write the equation for the budget set:

$$B = [x \in X : px \leq I]$$

Notice straightaway that the consumption space is now bounded from both below and above. See this in the two dimensional space. Consider Figure 1.12.

The budget set $B = p_1 X_1 + p_2 X_2 \leq I$. The hatched region is bounded from below by the boundary and (0, 0) and above from the income constraint. Notice that the budget set is closed and bounded, that is, it is compact.

Definition of a compact set: a set is compact if it is closed and bounded.

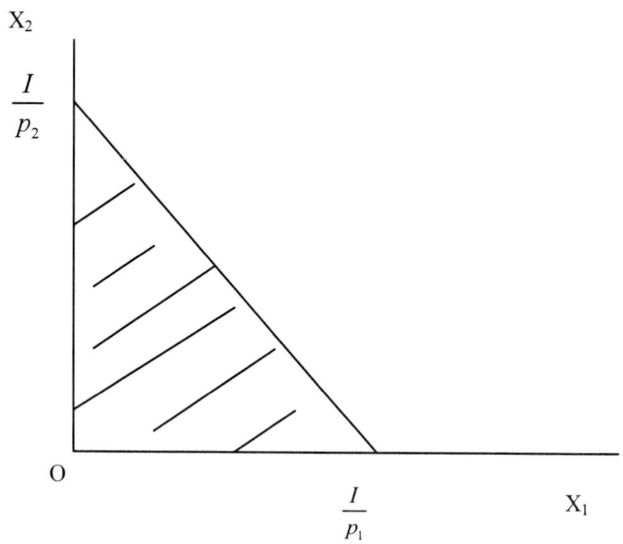

Figure 1.12

The utility maximization problem of the consumer can now be defined:

$$\underset{X_i}{Max} U(X_1, X_2, X_n)$$

Subject to

$$p_1X_1 + p_2X_2 + ... + p_nX_n \leq I$$
and $x \in X$.

This is a maximization problem and to show that a solution to this problem exists, we require the famous Weirstrauss theorem.

Weirstrauss theorem: this theorem states that a continuous function on a closed and bounded set will have a maximum or a minimum.

Importance of compact sets can be illustrated by a simple example. Consider a set, which is not closed like (0, 1). Let *f(x)* be *x*. This function has no maximum or minimum because there is no largest or smallest value. By our assumption we know that the utility function is continuous, hence, our maximization problem is well defined as:

$$\underset{X_i}{Max} U(X_1, X_2, ..., X_n)$$

Subject to

$$p_1X_1 + p_2X_2 + ... + p_nX_n = I$$

Note that the budget constraint holds as an equality because consumer prefers more to less. We are now solving for $X_i(i = 1...n)$ in terms of $p_i(i = 1...n)$ and nominal income. The solution $x_i = g(p_1...p_n, I)$ is known as the demand function and more precisely as the ordinary or Marshallian demand function. To carry out this maximization exercise, we use the Largrangian method of maximization. This method allows us to take account of the constraint which provides us with a compact set.

Let λ denote the undetermined Lagrange multiplier. Later on we shall show that λ denotes the marginal utility of income. Let us now set up our maximization problem with the help of the Lagrange method:

$$G = U[X_1, X_2, ..., X_n] - \lambda[p_1X_1 + p_2X_2 + ... + p_nX_n - I] \quad (1.1)$$

We take the first order partial derivatives of this with respect to our endogenous variables $X_1, X_2, ..., X_n$ and λ:

$$\frac{\partial G}{\partial X_1} = \frac{\partial U}{\partial X_1} - \lambda p_1 = 0 \quad (1.2)$$

$$\frac{\partial G}{\partial X_n} = \frac{\partial U}{\partial X_n} - \lambda p_n = 0 \quad (1.3)$$

$$\frac{\partial G}{\partial \lambda} = -[p_1 X_1 + p_2 X_2 + \ldots + p_n X_n - I] = 0 \qquad (1.4)$$

This gives us $n+1$ equations in $n+1$ unknowns in $X_1, X_2, \ldots, X_n$ and λ. Given that the system satisfies the conditions of Weirstrauss theorem, there exists a solution to the problem.

Consider the two commodities case:

$$G = U[X_1, X_2] - \lambda[p_1 X_1 + p_2 X_2 - I] \qquad (1.5)$$

$$\frac{\partial G}{\partial X_1} = \frac{\partial U}{\partial X_1} - \lambda p_1 = 0 \qquad (1.6)$$

$$\frac{\partial G}{\partial X_2} = \frac{\partial U}{\partial X_2} - \lambda p_2 = 0 \qquad (1.7)$$

$$\frac{\partial G}{\partial \lambda} = [p_1 X_1 + p_2 X_2 - I] = 0 \qquad (1.8)$$

Now from equations (1.6) and (1.7) we obtain:

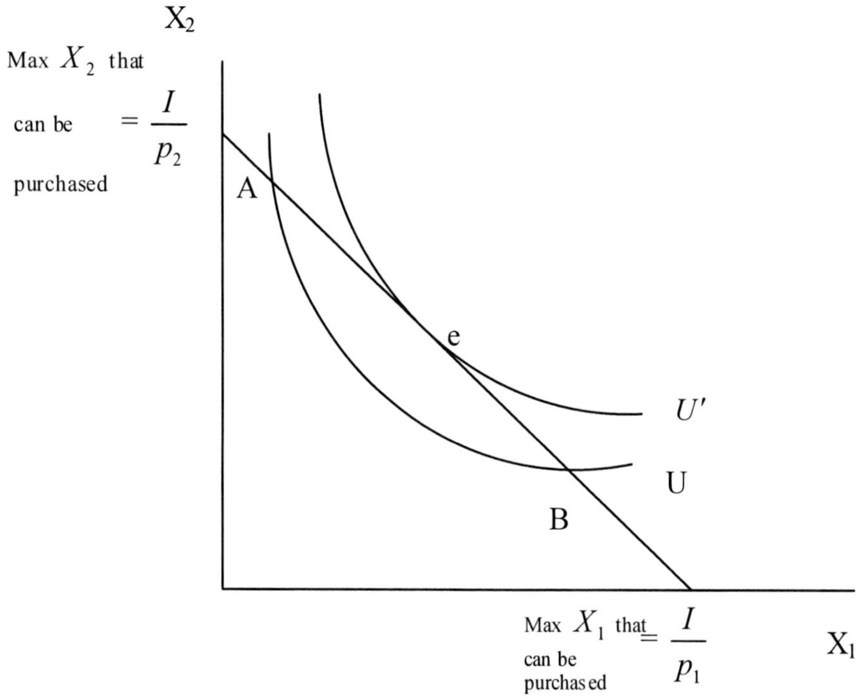

Figure 1.13

$$\frac{\partial U / \partial X_1}{\partial U / \partial X_2} = \frac{p_1}{p_2} \tag{1.9}$$

At the point of interior maximization, the ratio of marginal utilities is equal to the ratio of commodity prices. Let us analyze this condition below:

Why is it that point *A* and *B* are not equilibrium points? Let us analyze point *A*. At *A* the market rate of substitution is not equal to the subjective rate of substitution. Consider the following enlarged picture:

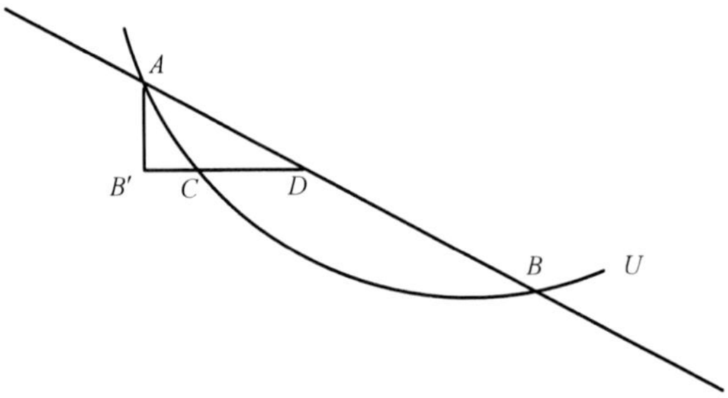

If the consumer gives up AB' of X_1, then to remain on the indifference curve he/she only requires $B'C$ of good X_1 but in the market he/she can obtain $B'D > B'C$. Therefore, there are arbitrage possibilities and the consumer will move to *D* and so on until it reaches point *e* on the indifference curve *U*.

We shall assume that the second order condition which states that:

$$h' D^2 U(X'X) h \leq 0 \text{ for all } h \text{ s.t. } ph=0 \tag{1.10}$$

We now construct the indirect utility function. By solving the first order condition for the demand functions we know that:

$$X_i = X_i[p_1 \ldots p_n, I] \tag{1.11}$$

Therefore the indirect utility function *V* is given by:

$$V = U\{X_1[p_1,\ldots,p_n,I], X_2[p_1,\ldots,p_n,I],\ldots,X_n[p_1,\ldots,p_n,I]\}$$

From this the indirect utility function can be written as:

$$V = V[p_1,\ldots,p_n,I] \tag{1.12}$$

or in vector notation

$$V = V[p, I] \tag{1.13}$$

where p denotes the vector of prices.

Before stating the properties of this function, we first show that λ is the marginal utility of income.

Proof:

we know that:

$$V = V[p_1,..., p_n, I] = U\{X_1[p_1,..., p_n, I], X_2[p_1,..., p_n, I],..., X_n[p_1,..., p_n, I]\}$$

Let us differentiate this with respect to nominal income I:

$$\frac{\partial V}{\partial I} = \frac{\partial V}{\partial X_1}\frac{\partial X_1}{\partial I} + ... + \frac{\partial V}{\partial X_n}\frac{\partial X_n}{\partial I} = \lambda p_1 \frac{\partial X_1}{\partial I} + ... + \lambda p_n \frac{\partial X_n}{\partial I} = \lambda\left[p_1 \frac{\partial X_1}{\partial I} + ... + p_n \frac{\partial X_n}{\partial I}\right] = \lambda$$

The bracketed term equals one.

Therefore λ is the marginal utility of income.

Properties of the Indirect utility function:

1). The indirect utility function is non-increasing in prices $(p_1, p_2,...p_N)$. This implies that indirect utility can not increase when prices increase. In similar manner, the indirect utility function is non-decreasing in income, that is, utility can not decrease when income rises.

2). The indirect utility function is homogenous of degree zero in prices and nominal income.

3). The indirect utility function is convex in prices.

4). The indirect utility function is continuous for all prices (strictly positive) and positive nominal income.

An easy way of proving some of these properties is by using calculus and taking first and second order derivatives of the indirect utility function.

The links between commodity and price space can be easily demonstrated by using direct and indirect indifference curves as shown in Figure 1.14.

$$p_1 X_1 + p_2 X_2 = I$$

We normalize prices so that $\overline{p}_1 = \frac{p_1}{I}$ and $\overline{p}_2 = \frac{p_2}{I}$.

Let $X_2 = 0$, then $\overline{p}_1 X_1 = 1$. In quadrant II we draw this curve, which gives all combinations of $\overline{p}_1 X_1$ such that they equal 1. Similarly in quadrant III, we draw all combinations of $\overline{p}_2 X_2$ such that they equal 1. Direct indifference curves in quadrant I show the level of welfare for the consumer in the commodity space while indirect indifference curves show the same information in the price space. Note that the worse than or as good as set in the price space is strictly convex demonstrating property 3 of the indirect utility function.

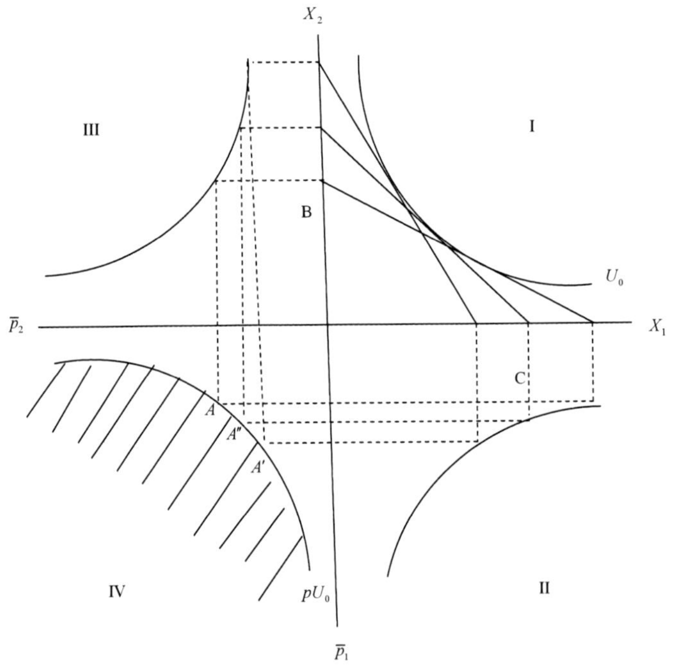

Figure 1.14

An example:
Consider a Cobb-Douglas utility function:

$$U = X_1^{1/2} X_2^{1/2}$$

Let us maximize this subject to a budget constraint $p_1 X_1 + p_2 X_2 = I$

$$G = X_1^{1/2} X_2^{1/2} - \lambda[p_1 X_1 + p_2 X_2 - I]$$

$$\frac{\partial G}{\partial X_1} = \frac{1}{2} X_1^{-1/2} X_2^{1/2} - \lambda p_1 = 0$$

$$\frac{\partial G}{\partial X_2} = \frac{1}{2} X_1^{1/2} X_2^{-1/2} - \lambda p_2 = 0$$

$$\frac{\partial G}{\partial \lambda} = -[p_1 X_1 + p_2 X_2 - I] = 0$$

The solutions to the above system provide the two Marshallian demand functions:

$$X_1^* = \frac{I}{2p_1}$$

$$X_2^* = \frac{I}{2p_2}$$

and the solution for the Lagrange multiplier is:

$$\lambda^* = \frac{1}{2}\left(\frac{p_1}{p_2}\right)^{\frac{1}{2}}$$

The indirect utility function for the Cobb-Douglas case is given below:

$$V = \frac{I}{2\sqrt{p_1 p_2}}$$

Now V is increasing in I and falling in p_1, p_2. By setting $I = 1$ we obtain that $V = \dfrac{1}{2\sqrt{p_1 p_2}}$, which is the equation for price indifference curve.

From above we can also generate an expenditure function. *The inverse of the indirect utility function is known as the expenditure function.* It is obtained by replacing income I by expenditure e and replacing V by U. Note that this technique utilizes the property that at the equilibrium point expenditure equals income. Hence, in the Cobb-Douglas case we obtain:

Indirect utility function: $V = \dfrac{I}{2\sqrt{p_1 p_2}}$

$$\therefore U = \frac{e}{2\sqrt{p_1 p_2}}$$

Expenditure function: $e = 2\sqrt{p_1 p_2}$

This is the Cobb-Douglas expenditure function.

The expenditure function is obtained from solving the following minimization problem.

Problem:

$$e = [p_1, p_2, ..., p_n, \overline{U}] = \min_{X_i} p_1 X_1 + p_2 X_2 + ... + p_n X_n$$

Subject to:

$$U[x_1, x_2, ..., x_n] = \overline{U}$$

The expenditure function gives the minimum expenditure (cost) to achieve a given level of utility. The expenditure function has the following properties:

1). Expenditure can not decrease when prices rise.
2). Expenditure function is homogeneous of degree 1 in prices.
3). The expenditure function is concave in prices.
4). The expenditure function is continuous in prices provided all prices are positive.

The Hicksian or compensated demand function is obtained in the following manner:

$$X_i^c = \frac{\partial e}{\partial p_i} \qquad \text{for } i = 1 \ldots n.$$

This is a simple application of the Envelope theorem. Note that we have drawn a distinction between a Hicksian (compensated) and a Marshallian (uncompensated) demand curve.

In figure below these curves are drawn. The consumer is at a point of initial equilibrium at point e_0 at the relative price (p_1 / p_2) given by the slope of the line *AB*. At this point both income and expenditure are equal. Moreover the consumer derives welfare level shown by U^*. Suppose the relative price of X_1 falls and is denoted by the slope of the line AB'. Then the consumer moves to point e_1. Now point e_0 and e_1 are represented in the space X_1 and p_1 / p_2 by points e_0' and e_1', which show the demand for X_1 at these relative prices. When we join these points we obtain the Marshallian demand curve. The compensated demand curve is obtained by moving AB' parallel such that it is tangential to the indifference curve U^* at point e_0'' giving a lower demand for X_1. The curve which goes through points e_0' and e_0'' is known as the compensated demand curve.

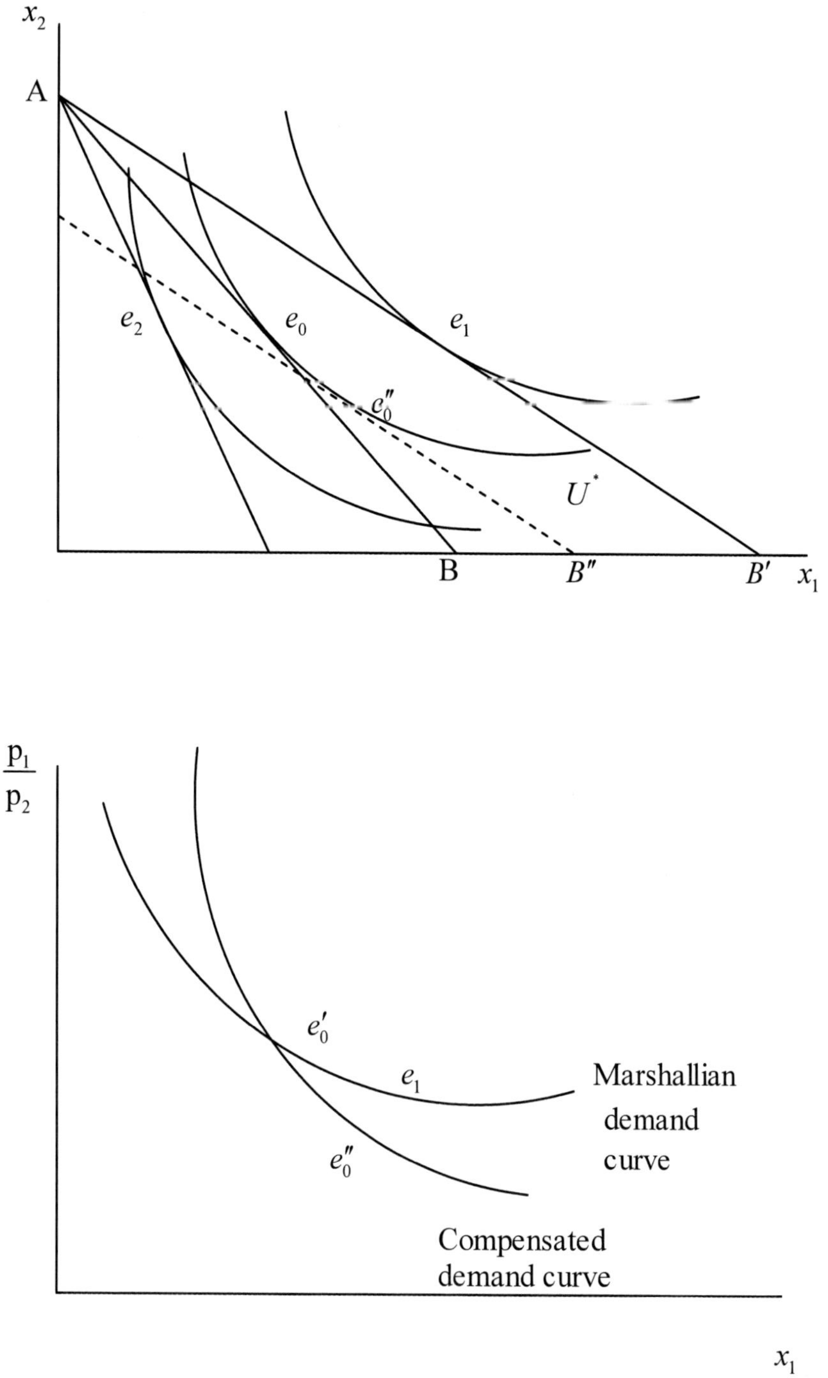

Figure 1.15

In obtaining this graph you can clearly see the important identities which relate to expenditure, income and utility. These are as follows:

(1) $e[p_1, p_2, ..., p_n, V(p_1, p_2, ..., p_n, I)] = I$. Expenditure and income are equal at point e_0.

(2) $V[p_1, p_2, ..., p_n, e(p_1, p_2, ..., p_n, I)] = V$. The maximum utility from expenditure $e[p_1, p_2, ..., p_n, V] = I$ is V^*.

(3) At point e_0 Marshallian and Hicksian demands are equal to each other.

(4) The compensated demand at utility level U^* is the same as the uncompensated demand at U^*.

We now proceed to show the importance of the indirect utility function. This importance is captured by Roy's identity.

Roy's identity. $$X_i[p_1, p_2, ..., p_n, I] = -\frac{\dfrac{\partial V(p_1, p_2, ..., p_n, I)}{\partial p_1}}{\dfrac{\partial V(p_1, p_2, ..., p_n, I)}{\partial I}}$$

Provided that $p_i > 0$ and $I > 0$.

Proof: The proof is developed by using the same technique we used to show that λ equals to the marginal utility of income. We know that:

$$V[p_1, p_2, ..., p_n, I] = V[X_1(p_1, p_2, ..., p_n, I), X_2(p_1, p_2, ..., p_n, I), ..., X_n(p_1, p_2, ..., p_n, I)]$$

Let us differentiate this, let us say with respect to price of good 2:

$$\frac{\partial V}{\partial p_2} = \frac{\partial V}{\partial X_1}\frac{\partial X_1}{\partial p_2} + \frac{\partial V}{\partial X_2}\frac{\partial X_2}{\partial p_2} + \frac{\partial V}{\partial X_3}\frac{\partial X_3}{\partial p_2} + ... + \frac{\partial V}{\partial X_n}\frac{\partial X_n}{\partial p_2}$$

We already know that:

$$\frac{\partial V}{\partial p_2} = \lambda\left[p_1\frac{\partial X_1}{\partial p_2} + p_2\frac{\partial X_2}{\partial p_2} + p_3\frac{\partial X_3}{\partial p_2} + ... + p_n\frac{\partial X_n}{\partial p_2}\right]$$

From the budget constraint:

$$p_1 X_1 + p_2 X_2 + ... + p_n X_n = I$$

It follows that:

$$p_1 \frac{\partial X_1}{\partial p_2} + X_2 + p_2 \frac{\partial X_2}{\partial p_2} + ... + p_n \frac{\partial X_n}{\partial p_2} = 0$$

It follows that:

$$\frac{\partial V}{\partial p_2} = -\lambda X_2(\ ) \qquad \text{(A)}$$

We also know that:

$$\frac{\partial V}{\partial I} = \lambda \qquad \text{(B)}$$

Combine (A) and (B):

$$X_2(\ ) = -\frac{\partial V / \partial p_2}{\partial V / \partial I}$$

Q.E D.

Notes:

1. Two approaches are generally taken to analyse consumer behaviour. The first takes tastes as given which are summarized in preferences. The second approach imposes restrictions directly on the behaviour. This is based on the weak axioms of revealed preference. We will stay with the more traditional approach of analyzing consumer choice.
2. Later in these lectures, examples will be given where completeness is not satisfied.

Chapter 2

MORE CONSUMPTION THEORY

In Chapter 1 the Mashallian and Hicksian demand functions were derived. We also introduced the concepts of ordering, indifference curve, direct and indirect utility and the expenditure function. The relations among these concepts were also established. We now proceed to do some comparative statics. Recall that in setting up the utility maximization problem we drew a distinction between exogenous and endogenous variables. The exogenous variables are p_1 p_2 and *I,* and endogenous X_1 X_2 and *U.* What are comparative statics? Comparative statics concern themselves with the effect of changes in exogenous variables on the equilibrium values of the endogenous variables. So we can vary, *I,* nominal income holding p_1 and p_2 constant and /or vary p_1 (or p_2) holding *I* constant or we can vary all the exogenous variables.

Let us begin by varying nominal income *I* holding p_1 and p_2 constant. Recall that the slope of the budget constraint is given by the ratio of prices p_1 / p_2. Since we are holding this constant a variation in nominal income always moves the budget constraint up or down in a parallel manner. This is shown in Figure 2.1.

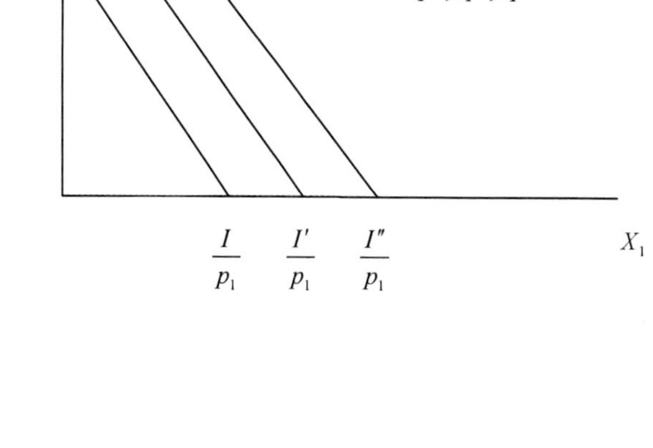

Figure 2.1

Each time the budget constraint shifts the consumer also has to find another position of utility maximization. Before showing this in terms of diagrams, let us define an income expansion path.

Definition Income Expansion Path shows the locus of utility maximization points when nominal income is varied at fixed prices.

From this we can also define the concept of an Engel curve. Let us consider again the space with which we work. This curve is defined in the commodities income space whereas the income expansion path is defined in the commodity space. Consider the income expansion paths shown in Figure 2.2.

Note something very important here. Consider the sign of $\frac{\partial X_1}{\partial I}$. It can be $\frac{\partial X_1}{\partial I} \gtreqless 0$. In spite of placing so many restrictions on consumer preferences and the consumption set, economic theory is unable to predict the sign of the income effect: it could be positive, zero or negative. Income effects are exceedingly important in many areas of economics and in particular, for analysing stability conditions. We now define two types of goods.

Normal goods: $\frac{\partial X_1}{\partial I} \geq 0$. Income effect for normal goods is non-negative.

Inferior goods: $\frac{\partial X_1}{\partial I} < 0$. Income effect for inferior goods is strictly negative.

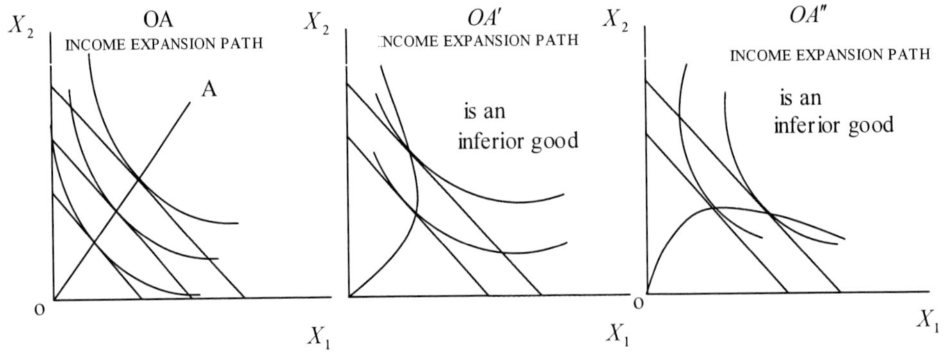

Figure 2.2

We now show an interesting result. We prove that all goods cannot be inferior implying that at least one good is normal in consumption.

Consider the budget constraint in the n good case:

$$p_1X_1 + p_2X_2 + ... + p_nX_n = I$$

Let us differentiate this with respect to nominal income at fixed prices to obtain:

$$p_1 \frac{\partial X_1}{\partial I} + p_2 \frac{\partial X_2}{\partial I} + \ldots + p_n \frac{\partial X_n}{\partial I} = 1$$

Since the right hand side of this is positive, therefore at least one of all $\frac{\partial X_i}{\partial I} > 0$.

Before deriving the Engel curve, let us introduce the concept of elasticity. Elasticity between any two variables is defined as the logarithmic differentiation of these variables, so:

$$\frac{d \log X}{d \log Y} = \frac{dX/X}{dY/Y} = \frac{Y}{X}\frac{dX}{dY}$$

Given the elasticity between the variables X and Y we can now define the elasticity of the Engel curve. In figure 2.3 we plot the Engel curve for the normal good case:

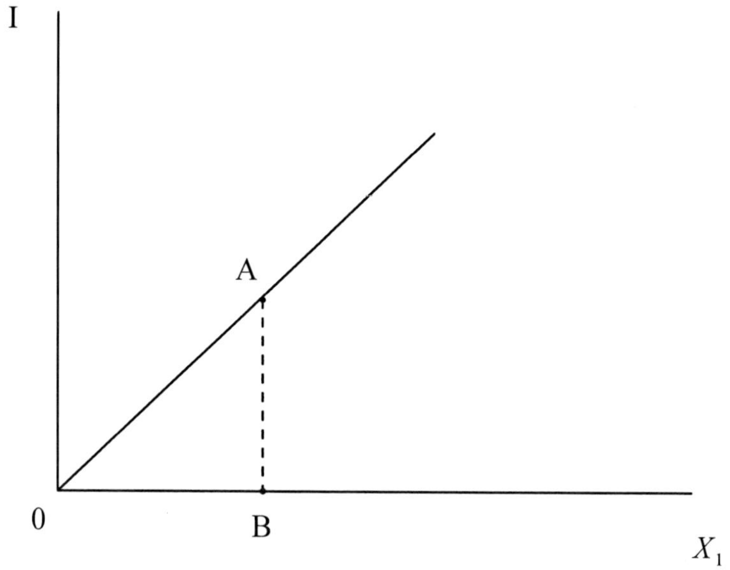

Figure 2.3

Let us consider elasticity at point A. The income elasticity at A is:

$$\eta = \frac{d \log X_1}{d \log I} = \frac{I}{X_1}\frac{dX_1}{dI} = \frac{AB}{OB}\frac{OB}{AB} = 1$$

Now consider another case.

In Figure 2.4, elasticity at point A is given by:

$$\eta = \frac{I}{X_1}\frac{dX_1}{dI} = \frac{AB}{OB}\frac{CB}{AB} = \frac{CB}{OB} < 1$$

By the method given above all elasticities can be measured geometrically. It is a very useful technique for visualizing elasticity geometrically and obtaining a visual representation of elasticity in many areas of economics.

Now consider varying p_1 and holding nominal income I constant. Note that real income in terms of p_1 now changes as this is defined as I/p_1 - a rise (fall) in p_1 lowers (increases) real income in terms of p_1. Consider the following figures:

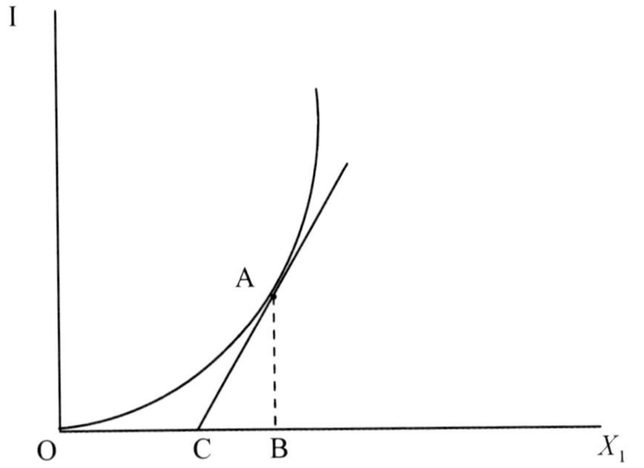

Figure 2.4

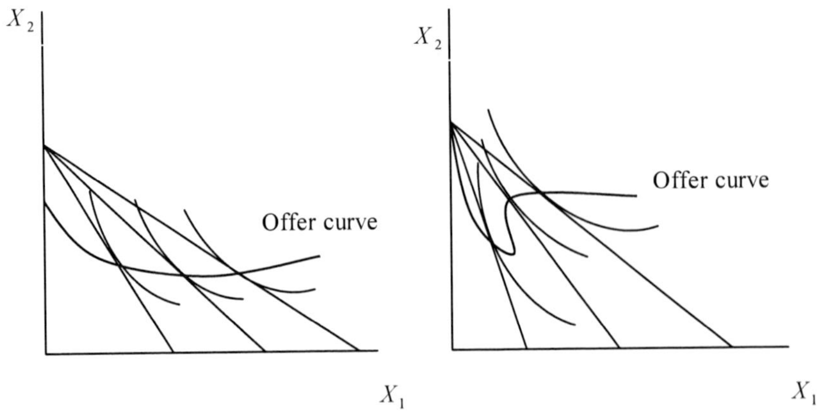

Figure 2.5

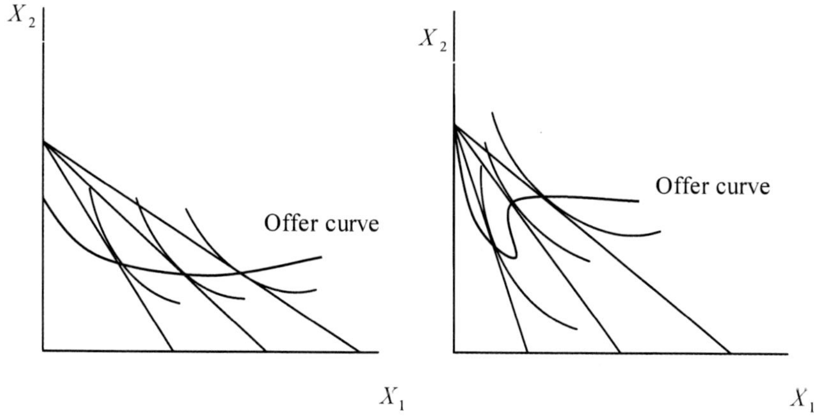

Figure 2.6

Notice that in the left hand side consumption of X_1 rises as the price of X_1 falls, while in the graph on the right hand side the amount of X_1 rises as its price falls. Such a good is known as a Giffen good. In both cases two effects are present. These are known as: substitution and income effects. Substitution effect is defined as movement in X_1 when its price changes at constant real income, while income effect is defined as the change in consumption of X_1 when nominal income changes at constant prices. As stated earlier that the assumptions and other restrictions on the consumer do not allow us to give a determinate sign to income effect, hence, income effect $\frac{\partial X_1}{\partial I} \gtreqless 0$ can be positive, zero or negative. In the case of Giffen goods income and substitution effects work in opposite direction. The substitution effect is always negative. The relation between these two effects is shown by the famous Slutsky equation. In essence it shows the link between compensated (Hicksian) and the uncompensated (Marshallian) demand curves. These are redrawn again for the purpose of showing the Slutsky equation.

The starting point of the proof of the Slutsky equation is point *e* where direct utility equals indirect utility, *U*=*V*, for the maximized utility bundle and expenditure equals income, *e*=*I*. Bearing this in mind we now write the proof of the Slutsky equation.

<u>Slutsky equation</u>: Statement:

$$\frac{\partial X_i[p_1, p_2, ..., p_n, I]}{\partial p_i} = \frac{\partial X_i^c[p_1, p_2, ..., p_n, I]}{\partial p_i} - \frac{\partial X_i}{\partial I} X_i[.]$$

<u>Proof</u>: Let $X^* = \left[X_1^*, X_2^*, ..., X_j^*, ..., X_n^*\right]$

It represents the bundle chosen at the point of utility maximization at prices $\left[p_1^*, p_2^*, ..., p_j^*, ..., p_n^*, I^*\right]$. Now we know from definition of point *e* that $U^* = U\left[X_1^*, X_2^*, ..., X_j^*, ..., X_n^*\right]$. We also know that at point *e*:

$$X_i^c\left[p_1^*, p_2^*, \ldots, p_i^*, \ldots, p_n^*, U^*\right] = X_i\left[p_1^*, p_2^*, \ldots, p_i^*, \ldots, p_n^*, I\right]$$

However, at point *e*, $I = e$, hence:

$$X_j^c\left[p_1^*, p_2^*, \ldots, p_j^*, \ldots, p_n^*, U^*\right] = X_j\left[p_1^*, p_2^*, \ldots, p_j^*, \ldots, p_n^*, e\left(p_1^*, p_2^*, \ldots, p_j^*, \ldots, p_n^*, U^*\right)\right]$$

Let us differentiate this with respect to p_i:

$$\frac{\partial X_j^c}{\partial p_i^*} = \frac{\partial X_j}{\partial p_i^*} + \frac{\partial X_j}{\partial e}\frac{\partial e}{\partial p_i^*} = \frac{\partial X_j}{\partial p_i^*} + \frac{\partial X_j}{\partial I}\frac{\partial I}{\partial p_i^*} = \frac{\partial X_j}{\partial p_i^*} + \frac{\partial X_j}{\partial I} X_j^*$$

Therefore:

$$\frac{\partial X_j}{\partial p_i^*} = \frac{\partial X_j^c}{\partial p_i^*} - \frac{\partial X_j}{\partial I} X_j^*$$

which shows the Slutsky equation.

In terms of Figure 2.6, we have drawn the compensated and uncompensated demand curves the movement from *e* to *A* which is decomposed as: from *e* to *B* by substitution effect and from *B* to *A* by income effect.

Example: Cobb-Douglas case:

$$V\left[p_1, p_2, I\right] = \frac{I}{\sqrt{p_1 p_2}}$$ indirect utility function

$$e\left[p_1, p_2, U\right] = U\sqrt{p_1 p_2}$$ expenditure function

$$X_1\left[p_1, p_2, I\right] = \frac{I}{2p_1}$$ ordinary demand curve

$$X_1^c\left[p_1, p_2, U\right] = \frac{U}{2}\sqrt{\frac{p_2}{p_1}}$$ compensated demand curve

$$\frac{\partial X_1}{\partial p_1} = -\frac{I}{2p_1^2}$$ slope of uncompensated demand curve

$$\frac{\partial X_1}{\partial I} = \frac{1}{2p_1}$$ Income effect

$$\frac{\partial X_1^c}{\partial p_1} = -\frac{Up_1^{-3/2} p_2^{1/2}}{4}$$ slope of compensated demand curve

Replace U by V to obtain:

$$\frac{\partial X_1^c}{\partial p_1} = -\frac{I \Big/ p_1^{1/2} p_2^{1/2}}{4p_1^{3/2} p_2^{1/2}} = -\frac{Ip_1^{-2}}{4} < 0$$

Now:

$$\frac{\partial X_1^c}{\partial p_1} - \frac{\partial X_1}{\partial I} X_1 = -\frac{Ip_1^{-2}}{4} - \frac{1}{2p_1}\frac{I}{p_1} = -\frac{I}{4p_1^2} - \frac{I}{4p_1^2} = -\frac{I}{2p_1^2} = \frac{\partial X_1}{\partial p_1}$$

So we have seen how the Slutsky equation operates for the Cobb-Douglas case.

Let us now state the properties of the demand function. These properties follow from the expenditure function. We show that the expenditure function is concave. Now a concave function is defined as:

$$f[\lambda X_1 + (1-\lambda)X_2] \geq \lambda f(X_1) + (1-\lambda) f(X_2)$$

Example:

Let

$$f(X) = X^{1/2}$$
$$X_1 = 4$$
$$X_2 = 25 \text{ and}$$
$$\lambda = 0.5$$

Then:

$$f[0.5(4) + 0.5(25)] \geq 0.5 f(4) + 0.5 f(25)$$
$$f[2 + 12.5] \geq 1 + 2.5$$
$$f[14.5] \geq 3.5$$
$$(14.5)^{1/2} \geq 3.5$$
$$3.807 > 3.5$$

A concave function is shown in Figure 2.7.

P.1: We know that the compensated demand function:

$$X_j^c = \frac{\partial e}{\partial p_j}$$

It follows that:

$$\frac{\partial X_j^c}{\partial p_j} = \frac{\partial^2 e}{\partial p_j^2}$$

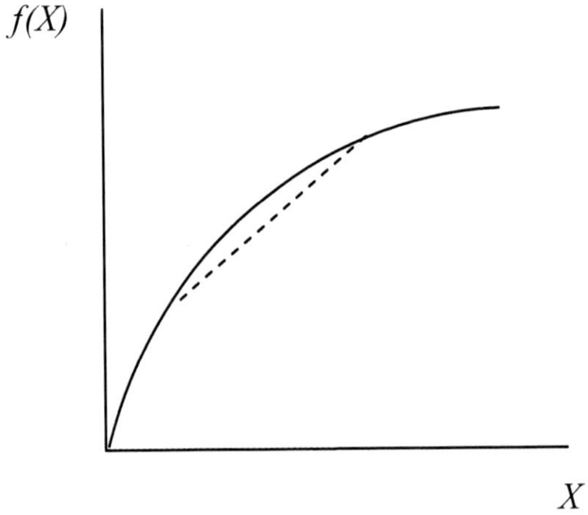

Figure 2.7

This gives us a matrix of substitution terms. Since e is a concave function it follows that the matrix of substitution terms is negative semi-definite.

P.2: The matrix of substitution terms is symmetric. The proof is trivial.

P.3: The substitution effect is non-positive. Follows straight from the concavity of the expenditure function.

P.4: The matrix $\left[\frac{\partial X_i[p_1, p_2, ..., p_n, I]}{\partial p_j} + \frac{\partial X_i}{\partial I} X_i\right]$ is a symmetric, negative semi-definite.

OLD FASHIONED WAY OF GENERATING THE SLUTSKY EQUATION

Although duality has been present in economics for a long time, to my knowledge, it only appeared in text books with Varian (1978). In the old days the Slutsky Equation used to be derived by using the first older conditions for utility maximization. This is shown below in the two good case. The first order conditions for the two good case are:

$$-p_1X_1 - p_2X_2 + I = 0$$
$$\frac{\partial U}{\partial X_1} - \lambda p_1 = 0$$
$$\frac{\partial U}{\partial X_2} - \lambda p_2 = 0$$

Let us differentiate this system with respect to p_1 and recall that U is a function of X_1 and X_2. We obtain:

$$-p_1\frac{\partial X_1}{\partial p_1} - p_2\frac{\partial X_2}{\partial p_1} = X_1$$
$$\frac{\partial^2 U}{\partial X_1^2}\frac{\partial X_1}{\partial p_1} + \frac{\partial^2 U}{\partial X_1 \partial X_2}\frac{\partial X_2}{\partial p_1} - \frac{\partial \lambda}{\partial p_1}p_1 = \lambda$$
$$\frac{\partial^2 U}{\partial X_2 \partial X_1}\frac{\partial X_1}{\partial p_1} + \frac{\partial^2 U}{\partial X_2^2}\frac{\partial X_2}{\partial p_1} - \frac{\partial \lambda}{\partial p_1}p_2 = 0$$

Or in matrix notation:

$$\begin{bmatrix} -p_1 & -p_2 & 0 \\ \dfrac{\partial^2 U}{\partial X_1^2} & \dfrac{\partial^2 U}{\partial X_1 \partial X_2} & -p_1 \\ \dfrac{\partial^2 U}{\partial X_2 \partial X_1} & \dfrac{\partial^2 U}{\partial X_2^2} & -p_2 \end{bmatrix} \begin{bmatrix} \dfrac{\partial X_1}{\partial p_1} \\ \dfrac{\partial X_2}{\partial p_1} \\ \dfrac{\partial \lambda}{\partial p_1} \end{bmatrix} = \begin{bmatrix} X_1 \\ \lambda \\ 0 \end{bmatrix}$$

By using the Cramer's rule we can solve this system. We will only solve for $\dfrac{\partial X_1}{\partial p_1}$:

$$\frac{\partial X_1}{\partial p_1} = \frac{\begin{vmatrix} X_1 & -p_2 & 0 \\ \lambda & \frac{\partial^2 U}{\partial X_1 \partial X_2} & -p_1 \\ 0 & \frac{\partial^2 U}{\partial X_2^2} & -p_2 \end{vmatrix}}{\begin{vmatrix} -p_1 & -p_2 & 0 \\ \frac{\partial^2 U}{\partial X_1^2} & \frac{\partial^2 U}{\partial X_1 \partial X_2} & -p_1 \\ \frac{\partial^2 U}{\partial X_2 \partial X_1} & \frac{\partial^2 U}{\partial X_2^2} & -p_2 \end{vmatrix}}$$

$$= \frac{X_1\left[-p_2 \frac{\partial^2 U}{\partial X_1 \partial X_2} + p_1 \frac{\partial^2 U}{\partial X_2^2}\right] - \lambda\left[-p_2^2\right]}{p_1\left[-\frac{\partial^2 U}{\partial X_1 \partial X_2} p_2 + p_1 \frac{\partial^2 U}{\partial X_2^2}\right] - p_2\left[-\frac{\partial^2 U}{\partial X_1^2} p_2 + p_1 \frac{\partial^2 U}{\partial X_2 \partial X_1}\right]}$$

By reorganizing terms:

$$\text{Let } D = p_1^2 \frac{\partial^2 U}{\partial X_2^2} + p_2^2 \frac{\partial^2 U}{\partial X_1^2} - 2 p_1 p_2 \frac{\partial^2 U}{\partial X_1 \partial X_2} < 0$$

$$\frac{\partial X_1}{\partial p_1} = \lambda \frac{p_2^2}{D} - \frac{X_1\left[-p_1 \frac{\partial^2 U}{\partial X_2^2} + p_2 \frac{\partial^2 U}{\partial X_1 \partial X_2}\right]}{D}$$

We shall now show that the second term is the income effect. Let us differentiate the system with respect to nominal income I holding p_1 and p_2 constant:

$$-p_1 \frac{\partial X_1}{\partial I} - p_2 \frac{\partial X_2}{\partial I} = 1$$

$$\frac{\partial^2 U}{\partial X_1^2} \frac{\partial X_1}{\partial I} + \frac{\partial^2 U}{\partial X_1 \partial X_2} \frac{\partial X_2}{\partial I} - \frac{\partial \lambda}{\partial I} p_1 = 0$$

$$\frac{\partial^2 U}{\partial X_2 \partial X_1} \frac{\partial X_1}{\partial I} + \frac{\partial^2 U}{\partial X_2^2} \frac{\partial X_2}{\partial I} - \frac{\partial \lambda}{\partial I} p_2 = 0$$

Note that D is the same. So we just have to solve for $\frac{\partial X_1}{\partial I}$. This equals:

$$\frac{\partial X_1}{\partial I} = \frac{\begin{vmatrix} -1 & -p_2 & 0 \\ 0 & \frac{\partial^2 U}{\partial X_1 \partial X_2} & -p_1 \\ 0 & \frac{\partial^2 U}{\partial X_2^2} & -p_2 \end{vmatrix}}{D} = \frac{-\left[-p_2 \frac{\partial^2 U}{\partial X_1 \partial X_2} + p_1 \frac{\partial^2 U}{\partial X_2^2}\right]}{D} = \frac{\left[-p_1 \frac{\partial^2 U}{\partial X_2^2} + p_2 \frac{\partial^2 U}{\partial X_1 \partial X_2}\right]}{D}$$

Hence:

$$\frac{\partial X_1}{\partial p_1} = \lambda \frac{p_2^2}{D} - X_1 \frac{\partial X_1}{\partial I}$$

First term is negative and it is the substitution effect. We have not proved this but it can be derived from the first order condition of the expenditure minimization problem.

Recall that we used a four quadrant diagram to represent direct and indirect indifference curves and established how easy it was to go from one space into another space, that is, from the commodity space to the price space and vice versa. Let us now show this formally. As in the graph we will assume that I=1 and prices are normalized. Consider the Cobb-Douglas case:

$$U = X_1^{1/2} X_2^{1/2}$$

$$X_1 = \frac{I}{2p_1} \qquad \text{since } I=1, \qquad X_1 = \frac{1}{2p_1}$$

$$X_2 = \frac{I}{2p_2} \qquad\qquad X_2 = \frac{1}{2p_2}$$

and

$$V = \frac{I}{2p_1 p_2} \qquad\qquad V = \frac{1}{2p_1 p_2}$$

Let us minimize the indirect utility function subject to the budget constraint.

$$\text{Min. } V = \frac{1}{2} \overline{p}_1^{-1/2} \overline{p}_2^{-1/2}$$

Subject to:

$$\bar{p}_1 X_1 + \bar{p}_2 X_2 = 1$$

where:

$$\bar{p}_1 = \frac{p_1}{I}$$

$$\bar{p}_2 = \frac{p_2}{I}$$

The Lagrange of this problem is:

$$L = \frac{1}{2}\bar{p}_1^{-1/2}\bar{p}_2^{-1/2} - \lambda\left[\bar{p}_1 X_1 + \bar{p}_2 X_2 - 1\right]$$

$$\frac{\partial L}{\partial p_1} = -\frac{1}{4}\bar{p}_1^{-3/2}\bar{p}_2^{-1/2} - \lambda X_1 = 0$$

$$\frac{\partial L}{\partial p_2} = -\frac{1}{4}\bar{p}_1^{-1/2}\bar{p}_2^{-3/2} - \lambda X_2 = 0$$

$$\frac{\partial L}{\partial \lambda} = -\bar{p}_1 X_1 - \bar{p}_2 X_2 + 1 = 0$$

By solving this system for $\bar{p}_1$ and $\bar{p}_2$, we obtain:

$$\bar{p}_1 = \frac{1}{2X_1} \quad \text{and} \quad \bar{p}_2 = \frac{1}{2X_2}$$

Hence:

$$V = \frac{1}{2p_1^{1/2}p_2^{1/2}} = \frac{1}{2\sqrt{\frac{1}{2X_1}}\sqrt{\frac{1}{2X_2}}} = X_1^{1/2}X_2^{1/2} = U$$

The Cobb Douglas case provides a very neat example of the application of duality.

REVEALED PREFERENCE

In all these lectures so far, for we have built demand theory on the basis of the properties of sets and orderings. It is the axiomatic approach to demand theory. However, there is another way of deriving the important result that the compensated demand curve slopes downwards. This approach is based on the behavioral properties of the consumer and is associated with Samuelson. Consider the following budget sets.

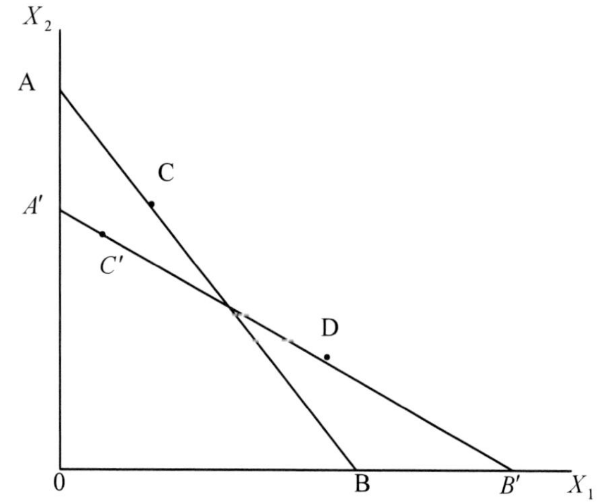

Figure 2.8

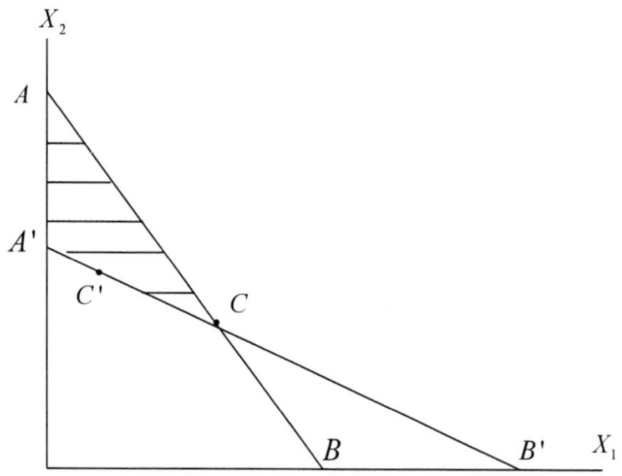

Figure 2.9

Suppose that the consumer faces the budget constraint AB at some nominal income I and prices given by the slope of the line AB. On this budget constraint the consumer chooses point C. Samuelson would say that C is revealed to be preferred to all points that belong to the consumption set OAB. Note that we have not drawn any indifference curves or said anything about consumer's preferences. Now consider another budget constraint and consumption set given by $OA'B'$. This consumer should not choose point C' as C' was available at income given by AB and prices associated with the budget constraint AB and the consumer had rejected it. Now consider a point D. We can not rank point D against point C by the revealed preference approach. Although these points could be ranked under the indifference curve approach. Now consider another budget constraint given by $A'B'$ in Figure 2.9. Suppose that point C is available both at the original set of prices given by the slope of the line AB and also at the set of prices given by the slope of the line $A''B''$ as shown in Figure 2.9. We know that all points in the area $AC'C$ are inferior to C as the consumer revealed that C was the preferred point. However, C can not be ranked with points that belong to the set $CB''A''$. We can now state that weak axiom of revealed preference.

Weak Axiom of Revealed Preference (WARP): If C and C' are feasible and C is chosen then at any set of prices and income where both C and C' are available the consumer will choose C to C'.

This axiom states two things. First, consumers choose what they prefer. Second, choices are stable and consistent. Rejected bundles are not chosen.

There also exists a stronger form of this axiom. It states that:

Strong Axiom of Revealed Preference (SARP): If commodity bundle A is preferred to B and B to C and so on. Then bundle C can not be revealed to be preferred to A.

Note that SARP is WARP with a transitivity condition.

The beautiful thing about WARP is that we can obtain the substitution effect from this simple property. Moreover, it also provides the foundation for constructing indices used in measuring gross national product and so on.

We now proceed to construct a proof based on WARP that the compensated demand curve is downward sloping.

Consider Figure 2.10. Consider two bundles A and B at prices given by the slopes of ZZ and $Z'\,Z'$. Let these prices be denoted by $((p_1^A, p_2^A)$ and (p_1^B, p_2^B). Further the consumer informs us that:

AIB

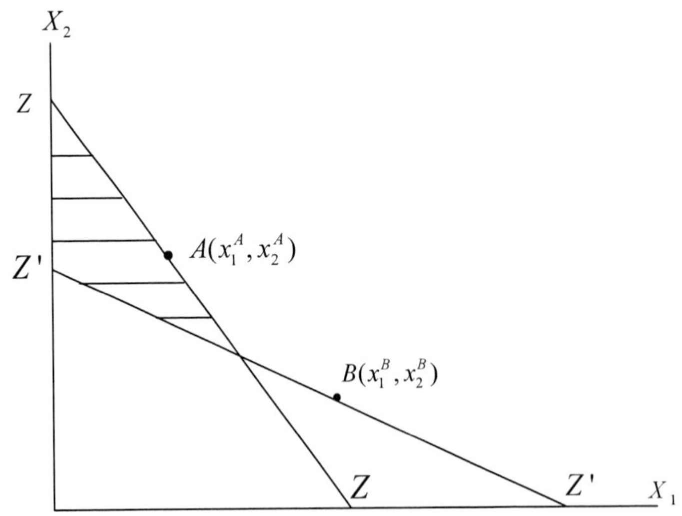

Figure 2.10

Note that we do not have to draw an indifference curve. We do not require that points A and B are connected by some sort of a curve. Now the proof runs along the following lines. First let us construct value bundles. These are:

$$p_1^A X_1^A, p_2^A X_2^A, p_1^A X_1^B, p_2^A X_2^B$$
$$p_1^B X_1^B, p_2^B X_2^B, p_1^B X_1^A, p_2^B X_2^B$$

This simply shows how to evaluate the bundles at different prices. Now by WARP:

$$p_1^A X_1^A + p_2^A X_2^A \le p_1^A X_1^B + p_2^A X_2^B \text{ since } A \text{ is chosen.}$$
$$p_1^B X_1^B + p_2^B X_2^B \le p_1^B X_1^A + p_2^B X_2^B$$

By addition we obtain:

$$p_1^A X_1^A + p_2^A X_2^A + p_1^B X_1^B + p_2^B X_2^B \le p_1^B X_1^A + p_2^B X_2^B + p_1^A X_1^B + p_2^A X_2^B$$
$$p_1^A\left(X_1^A - X_1^B\right) + p_2^A\left(X_2^A - X_2^B\right) + p_1^B\left(X_1^B - X_1^A\right) + p_2^B\left(X_2^B - X_2^A\right) \le 0$$

Therefore:

$$p_1^A\left(X_1^A - X_1^B\right) - p_1^B\left(X_1^A - X_1^B\right) + p_2^A\left(X_2^A - X_2^B\right) - p_2^B\left(X_2^A - X_2^B\right) \le 0$$
$$\left(p_1^A - p_1^B\right)\left(X_1^A - X_1^B\right) + \left(p_2^A - p_2^B\right)\left(X_2^A - X_2^B\right) \le 0$$

Now suppose that only price of commodity one changes then:

$$\left(p_1^A - p_1^B\right)\left(X_1^A - X_1^B\right) \le 0$$

which is nothing other than $\dfrac{\partial X_1}{\partial p_1} \le 0$ at constant utility as $A\ I\ B$.

Hence, we obtain the non-negativity of the substitution effect without assuming diminishing marginal rate of substitution.

Chapter 3

One Input-One Output Model for Theory of Production

The objective of this Chapter is to provide a simple and geometrical treatment of the neoclassical theory of the firm. This treatment is based on the one-input and one-output case. From this one-by-one model, the unconditional input demand function, the supply curve, profit function and the wage-profit frontier are derived. These concepts are used in many areas of economics. Difficult concepts associated with duality theory and rigorously derived by Varian (1984) and several other economists are presented in an intuitive and compact manner. The use of the one-input and one-output case simplifies the derivation of the unconditional input demand function, profit function supply curve and the wage-profit frontier because elementary geometry can be used for this purpose. An example of these concepts based on a simple production function is also developed. The firm is assumed to maximize profits and the use of isoprofit curves with the production function helps us in deriving all the above functions or graphs.

Modern Approach to Production Theory

We begin by distinguishing between inputs and outputs. Inputs are used to produce an output, for example, labour is used to produce rice.

We now introduce the concept of a production set. Since we are in a one-input one-output framework we let y denote output and L denote an input (labour). The set of all production vectors that constitute feasible plans is known as a product set and is denoted by $Y \in R^2$. Any $y \in Y$ is feasible.

We now define an input requirement set *IRS*.

Input Requirement Set (IRS)

The input requirement set for producing y^* units of output is the collection of all inputs that produce at least y^* units of output.

The *IRS* for output y^* is illustrated by the thick set line beginning at *A* in Figure 3.1. All the points on the thick line are capable of producing y^*. To derive neat solutions, we impose some restriction on this *IRS*. The first restriction is known as regularity.

REGULARITY

The input requirement set is closed and non-empty.

The meaning of the above condition is the following. First, the term "non-empty" means that there is some way of producing any level of output. Obviously a producer cannot operate if the *IRS* is empty because then there is no way of transforming inputs into outputs – hence the need for regularity. Second, closed means that the boundary of the set belongs to the set. The IRS in Figure 3.1 is regular.

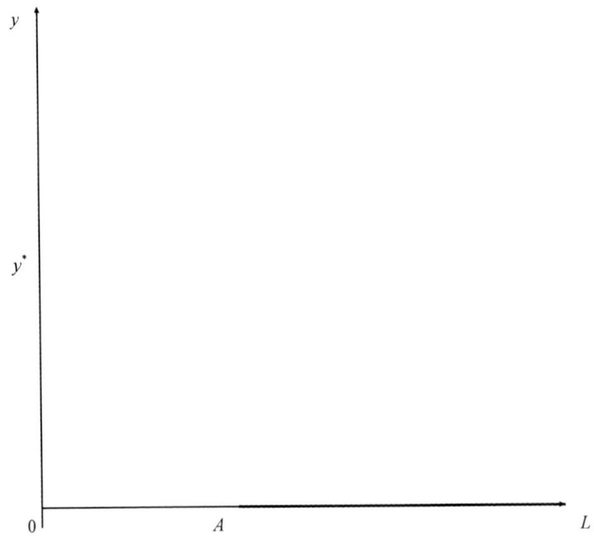

Figure 3.1. Input requirement set

MONOTONICITY

If a given output y^* can be produced by the use of a certain amount of input, then we can also produce y^* by using more of that input.

The meaning of the above assumption is obvious.

Finally we impose the restriction of convexity.

CONVEXITY

The input requirement set is convex.

The above restriction means that all linear combinations of any two points on the boundary set belong to the set. This is satisfied by the input of the requirement set in Figure 3.1.

PRODUCTION FUNCTION

Given all of the above restrictions on the *IRS*, we are now in a position to define a production function. A production function is defined as the relationship that associates a maximum output with given inputs.

$$y = F(L)$$

Where output y is a function of input labour and this transformation only chooses efficient points.

A few remarks are in order as $y = F(L)$. It is being assumed that:

$$y = F(0) = 0$$

implying that there is no free lunch. It is not possible to produce something from nothing. Also note that $O \in Y$, therefore, there is the possibility of inaction. The area under *OF* represents the production set.

The production function $y = F(L)$ is assumed to be twice differentiable and we assume that:

$$F'(L) > 0$$

and

$$F''(L) < 0$$

so that the production function is strictly concave.

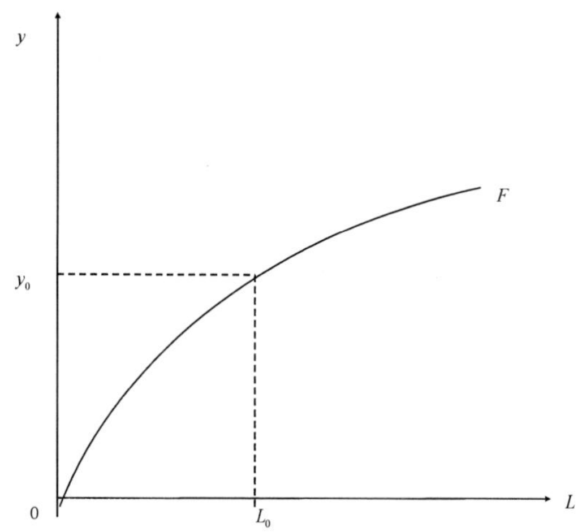

Figure 3.2. A Production Function

Let us draw a graph of the production function in the one-input one-output case. In Figure 3.2 on the horizontal axis we plot the amount of input (assumed to be labour). On the vertical axis the output y is plotted. The curve OF represents the production function which defines the maximum amount of output that can be produced from a given amount of labour input. Suppose the firm chooses L_0 as the labour input. Then by using L_0 units of labour it obtains output y_0. In a similar manner all other points on the curve OF can be interpreted. Note that this technology satisfies all the restrictions that we have imposed.

Statement of the Problem

Following the neoclassical traditions, we shall assume that the firm is a profit-maximizer. A firm produces a single output, y, from using a single input, labour (L). To obtain the optimal input and output points, we now set up the firm's profit maximization problem. It is important to distinguish between competitive and non-competitive markets before setting up the problem. In a competitive market the firm takes prices (both input and output) as given from outside. In non-competitive markets the firm is a price maker. Assuming that the firm operates in a competitive market, it takes the output price and factor price to be given from outside. These are denoted by P and w respectively. Given this information, the maximization froblem is written as follows:

$$\pi = py - wL \quad (3.1)$$

where py denotes total revenue and wL total cost. The term π denotes profit.

To solve the firm's choice problem geometrically, we shall introduce the concept of an isoprofit line.

Isoprofit Line: It shows combinations of output y and labour L that yield the same profit. An isoprofit line in real terms is defined below:

$$\frac{\bar{\pi}}{p} = y - \frac{wL}{p} \quad (3.2)$$

where $\frac{\bar{\pi}}{p}$ is a fixed level of real profit. The same exercise can also be conducted in nominal terms.

Since w and p are exogenously given to the firm, the above equation describes all combinations of L and y that are necessary to generate a fixed level of real profit. The isoprofit line is shown in Figure 3.3. It is clear that the intercept and slope of the isoprofit line are the real profit and real wage rate, respectively.

VARIATION IN ISOPROFIT CURVES

Recall that in deriving the isoprofit curve the following variables were given constant values: the magnitude of real profit and the real wage rate. In the case of neoclassical theory of consumer, variations in the budget line arise from changes in prices and/or income. Similarly, in the theory of the firm, changes in the isoprofit curve arise from changes in real wage and/or a change in real profit.

In Figure 3.3 different isoprofit curves for a constant real wage are also drawn. These are $\overline{\Pi}/P_0$ and $\overline{\Pi}/P_1$. They have the same slope which implies that the real wage is held constant – thus they are parallel to each other. Real profit along each one of these curves is constant. The isoprofit curves provide a complete analogy to a consumer's budget lines for different nominal incomes at fixed prices.

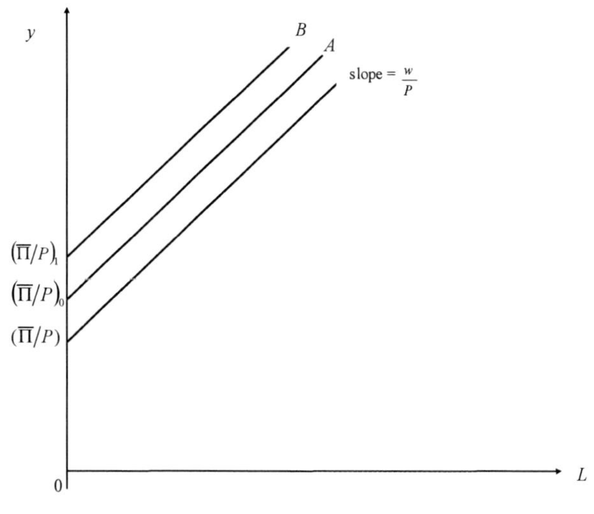

Figure 3.3. An Isoprofit Line

Let us now consider the impact of a change in the real wage rate on the isoprofit curve. The real wage can vary either through a change in w and/or p. Suppose that w increases while p remains fixed. Since the slope of the isoprofit curve is the real wage rate, a rise in w alone will increase the slope of the isoprofit lines as shown in Figure 3.4. This is equivalent to a movement in the consumer's budget line at fixed nominal income but different prices.

PROFIT-MAXIMIZING EQUILIBRIUM

We are now in a position to obtain the profit-maximizing equilibrium of the firm. To attain this equilibrium, the firm has to combine the knowledge of its technology with the market information contained in the isoprofit curve regarding market prices. In Figure 3.5 we illustrate the profit-maximizing point for a firm. On the horizontal axis we represent labour, L, and on the vertical axis output y. The production function is drawn as OF. Three isoprofit curves are drawn: AB, $A'B'$ and $A''B''$. They represent different levels of profit: on curve AB real profit equals OA; on curve $A'B'$ real profit equals OA' and on curve $A''B''$ real profit equals OA''.

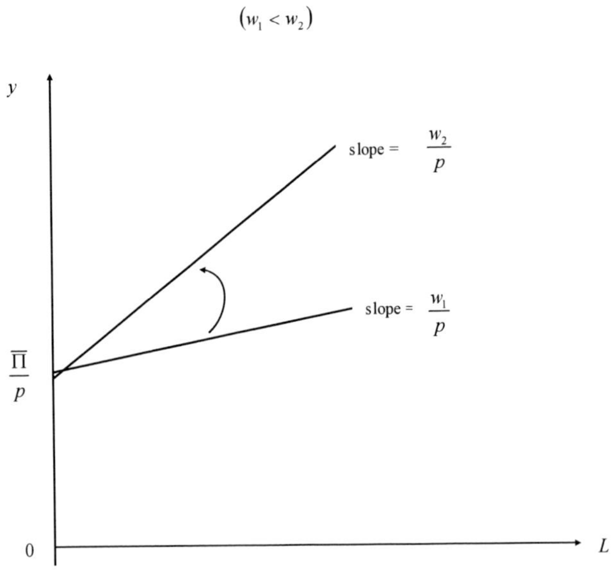

Figure 3.4. Isoprofit lines at different real wages

The firm is interested in choosing a point that maximizes profit. Graphically it means that the firm has to choose a point on *OF* that also belongs to the highest isoprofit line. Should it choose a point on AB? The answer is no because it can do better. Should it choose a point on $A''B''$? The answer is again no because the firm cannot produce on any point on $A''B''$. Thus the firm's solution is found by selecting a point at which the isoprofit curve is tangential to the production function *OF*. This point is denoted by *e*. At this equilibrium point, the firm hires OL^* of labour, produces Oy^* of output and makes a real profit of OA'. Thus, the principle of profit maximization allows the firm to arrive at its decision regarding the quantity of output it produces and the amount of labour it hires. It also determines the magnitude of profit the firm makes. In a competitive setting, firms only choose quantities of labour input and output such that profit is maximized. In consumer theory the individual consumer chooses the quantities of goods subject to a budget constraint. Note that for the firm the constraint is represented by the technology.

It is important at this stage to discuss the significance of the tangency condition. At the point of equilibrium the slope of the production function equals the slope of the isoprofit line. Note that the slope of the isoprofit line is the real wage rate (w/p) and that the slope of the production function measures the physical marginal product of labour *(MpL)*. Thus at the point of equilibrium:

$$\frac{w}{p} = MpL \text{ or } w = pMpL \tag{3.3}$$

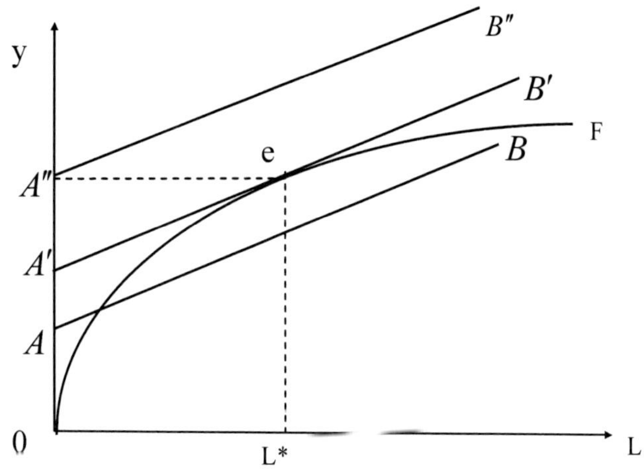

Figure 3.5. Profit-maximizing equilibrium

Thus at the point of profit-maximizing equilibrium, the labour hired should receive the value of its marginal product denoted by *pMpL*, that is, the marginal physical product of labour multiplied by the commodity price.

It is also useful to draw some similarities and differences between the consumer's utility-maximizing problem and the firm's profit-maximizing problem. The firm's technology as described by its production function and is the counterpart of consumer's preferences as captured by the utility function. The firm's isoprofit line is analogous (but not totally analogous) to the consumer's budget line. However, in the consumer theory, maximizing utility is the objective and the budget line acts as a constraint.

Derivation of the Input Demand Function

In Figure 3.6 we provide a simple method of obtaining an unconditional input demand function. An unconditional input demand function shows the quantities of input that a firm wishes to purchase at various input prices. In our case the input is labour, *L*, and the price of this input is the real wage rate, *w/P*.

We consider the top panel of Figure 3.6 first. Three isoprofit lines have been drawn for different wage rates as shown by the slope of lines ZZ, $Z'Z'$ and $Z''Z''$. In the lower panel for the three real wage rates under consideration, they are respectively shown by $(w/P)_0$, $(w/P)_1$ and $(w/P)_2$, where $(w/P)_0 > (w/P)_1 > (w/P)_2$. At these points the firm wishes to purchase *OA*, *OB* and *OC* units of labour, respectively. These points are transferred to the lower panel. For example, point *OA* in the top panel is translated to *OA* in the lower panel. By following the above procedure, we obtain the unconditional input demand function $L_D L_D'$. Note that the unconditional input demand curve is simply the *MpL* curve and is equivalent to the ordinary demand curve.

Note the following features of the input demand function. First, it is downward-sloping, i.e. as the real wage falls, the demand for labour increases. Second, each point on this input demand function is a point of profit maximization for the firm.

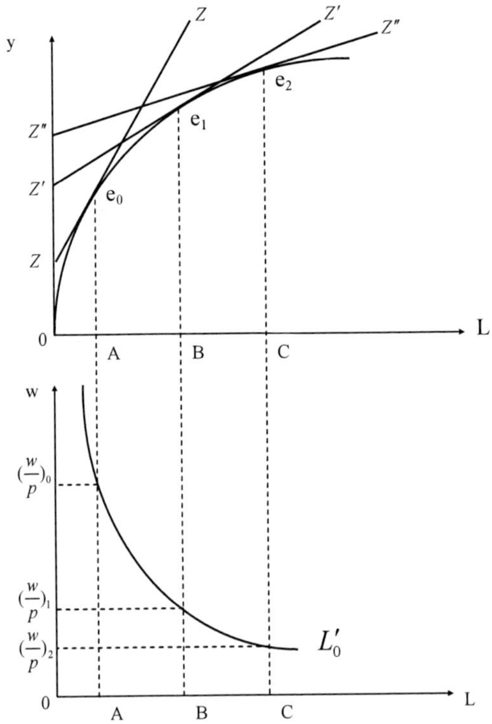

Figure 3.6. Derivation of a firm's input demand curve

Hence, at each point the value of the marginal product equals the real wage rate. Finally, the demand for input is derived from the demand for its output as represented in the top panel.

DERIVATION OF A SUPPLY CURVE

Recall that in the isoprofit curve we have a term $(w/P)L$. In the previous section we varied (w/P) to derive the input demand function. In this section we shall only vary P at a constant w to obtain the supply function which shows various levels of output that the firm wishes to produce at different commodity prices. This can be achieved by using the geometrical apparatus developed so far.

In the top panel of Figure 3.7 we have changed the axis from the previous diagrams. On the horizontal axis we now have output y and on the vertical axis labour, L. Thus, the production function OF is drawn in Figure 3.7 with axes switched. The slopes of the three lines AB, $A'B'$ and $A''B''$ represent three different levels of the commodity price. The price of y is lower on AB than on $A'B'$ and similarly it is lower on $A'B'$ than on $A''B''$. In other words, the price of y is increasing as we move from price line AB to $A'B'$ and to $A''B''$.

At the price given by the slope of AB (price equals P_0) output level y_0 is produced. This is plotted as the combination of y_0 and P_0 in the lower panel. This gives us point S on the firm's supply curve. In a similar manner point S' is obtained. The locus of points such as S and S' provides us with the supply curve of the firm. We note that the firm's output supply curve is necessarily upward-sloping and at each point of this curve the firm is maximizing its profit. The upward sloping supply curve in this case is a function of diminishing return to labour.

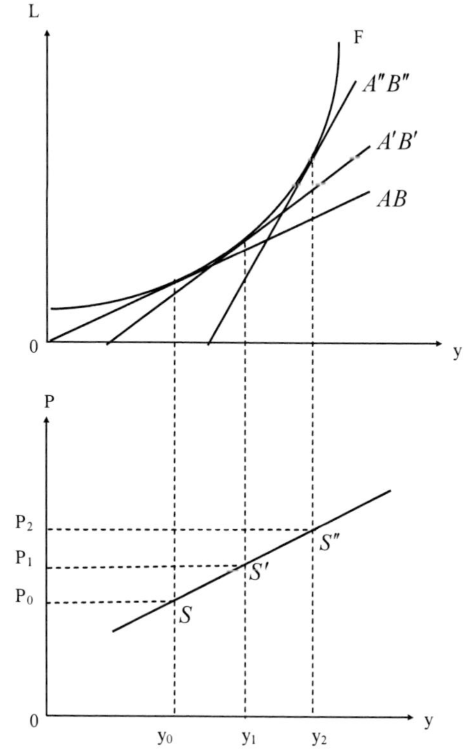

Figure 3.7. Derivation of a firm's supply curve

DERIVATION OF THE WAGE-PROFIT FRONTIER

In this section we shall vary the real wage w/p to obtain the wage-profit frontier which shows all equilibrium combinations of real wage w/p and real profit π/p. The problem is essentially to find a transformation that maps the firm's equilibrium point in the input-output space to a point in the real wage-real profit space. It is nice to see the link between the physical and price space. This can be easily done by combining the production function curve, isoprofit lines and the unconditional input demand function that has been derived in Section 4. In Figure 3.8 all four quadrants are utilized. The production function curve *OF* and the isoprofit lines are plotted in the first quadrant. In the second quadrant we draw a 45° line passing through the origin while the unconditional input demand curve is graphed in the fourth quadrant. Note that the real profit and real wage rate are plotted on the horizontal and vertical axes of the third quadrant, respectively.

Consider the isoprofit curve Ae_O which gives rise to equilibrium at e and the real profit is given by OA and real wage by the slope of Ae_O. The real profit OA is translated to OA' in the real profit axis via the 45° line in the second quadrant. At the equilibrium e_O the firm hires OL_O units of labour which corresponds to a real wage of OB' (slope of Ae_O) which can be read from the unconditional labour demand curve. The coordinates OA' and OB' define a point f_O in the real wage-real profit quadrant which corresponds to the equilibrium e_O in the input-output space. Similarly, the equilibrium point e_1 corresponding to the isoprofit line ce_1 is mapped to point f_1 in the real wage-real profit space. By following this procedure we can trace out the unconditional wage-profit frontier in the fourth quadrant of Figure 3.8.

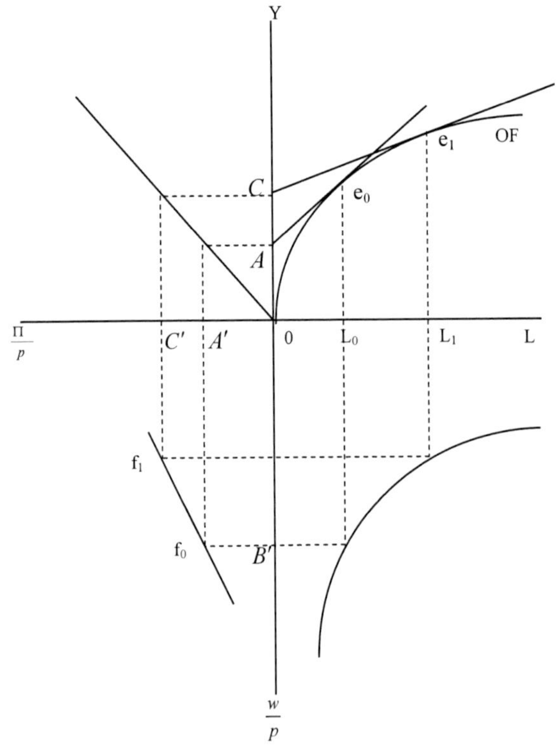

Figure 3.8. Derivation of a wage-profit frontier

Since profit can be thought of as the return to the owner of the firm, the unconditional wage-profit frontier is completely equivalent to the factor reward frontier discussed in a more advanced course of trade theory. Like the input demand and supply functions obtained previously, the wage-profit frontier is downward sloping, i.e. as the real wage increases real profit declines. Further, each point on the wage-profit frontier represents a profit-maximizing equilibrium for the firm. It shows conflict between the interest of workers and profit earners.

An example of the concepts is discussed below. Consider the following production function:

$$y = L^{1/2},\ y = F(L)\ \ F'(L) > 0, F''(L) < 0 \tag{3.4}$$

where y denotes output and L input of labour. This function has a positive first derivative and a negative second derivative. The firm's profit maximization problem can now be written as:

$$\underset{L}{Max}\ \Pi = py - wL = pL^{1/2} - wL \tag{3.5}$$

or in abstract terms:

$$\underset{L}{Max}\ \Pi = pF(L) - wL$$

Note that the firm takes prices both in the commodity and factor markets as given and maximizes over L. We differentiate Π with respect to L and set the first derivatives equal to zero:

$$\frac{\delta\Pi}{\delta L} = \frac{1}{2}pL^{-1/2} - w = 0, pF'(L) - w = 0 \tag{3.6}$$

or

$$\frac{p}{2L^{1/2}} = w$$

This states that at the point of profit-maximizing equilibrium the value of the marginal product equals the wage rate. Equation 3.4 can be solved for the unconditional input demand function which is given below:

$$L^* = \frac{1}{4}\left(\frac{p}{w}\right)^2, L^* = g\left(\frac{p}{w}\right) \tag{3.7}$$

It is clear that L^* is increasing in output price p and falling in input price w. Also observe that every point on the input demand function is a point of profit maximization.

By substituting the unconditional input demand function into equation (3.4) we obtain the supply function:

$$y^* = \frac{1}{2}\frac{p}{w}, y^* = y\left(\frac{p}{w}\right) \tag{3.8}$$

It is obvious that y^* is increasing in output price p implying that the supply curve is upward sloping for a given wage rate. Also note that y^* is falling in w. Again every point on the supply curve is a point of profit maximization.

The profit function is obtained by substituting the input demand function in the profit-maximizing problem. By carrying out this substitution and simplifying we obtain:

$$\Pi = \frac{p^2}{4w}, \Pi = \Pi(p, w) \tag{3.9}$$

This function is continuous, convex in p and its derivatives with respect to p and w provide the supply and input demand functions respectively.

$$\frac{\delta\Pi}{\delta p} = \frac{p}{2w} \quad \text{(supply curve)}$$

$$\frac{\delta\Pi}{\delta w} = \frac{p^2}{4w^2} \quad \text{(input demand function)}$$

Finally, the wage profit frontier has a negative slope as shown by differentiating equation (3.9) with respect to w, holding p constant:

$$\frac{d\Pi}{dw} = -\frac{\Pi}{w} \tag{3.10}$$

In this chapter we have presented a simple geometrical approach to the theory of the firm with duality and derived the unconditional input demand function; the supply curve, profit function and the wage-profit frontier.

Chapter 4

MORE GENERAL PRODUCTION THEORY

In Chapter 3 we have treated in great detail many important concepts and ideas involved in production theory on the basis of one input – one output case. It is time to move on to a more general case. Let us start by generalizing our definitions:

Definition Production Plan: A production plan $Y = [y_1, y_2, ..., y_n]$ is a vector of net outputs.

This is the most general way of defining the concept. In this definition an input is denoted by $y_i < 0$ and output by $y_i > 0$. This can be very confusing for many students and at some stage we will drop this convention and just clearly distinguish between inputs and outputs without resorting to so much generality. The advantage of working with the general definition is that one does not have to distinguish between inputs and outputs in advance.

Definition Production set: The set of all feasible plans of the firm is defined as a production set *Y*.

In the one input – one output case it is shown in Figure 4.1. Notation is being used from Chapter 3.

To avoid the problems of joint production we will restrict ourselves to the one output case and allow the number of inputs to be expanded. Let *y* denote output and V_i denote the *i*th input. Lower case *V* denotes the vector of inputs. We now generalize the definition of the input requirement set.

Definition Input Requirement Set (IRS):

$$G(y) = \{x \in R^n : (y_1, -V) \varepsilon Y\}$$

This states that the vector of input *V* belongs to the *n* dimensional Euclidean space to produce <u>at least</u> *y* and that the output *y* and vector *V* belong to the production plan.

In elementary microeconomics an isoquant is defined as the combination of labour and capital which produces a given level of output. We now state this idea in a more sophisticated manner.

$$I(y) = \{V \in R^n : V \varepsilon G(y) \text{ and } V \notin G(y) \text{ if } y' > y\}$$

It states that we only consider those inputs from the input requirement set that produce exactly y. Before providing any intuition about these concepts let us define a production function in more general notation.

Production Function:

$$G(V) = \{\, y \in R : y \text{ is the maximum output associated with } -V \in Y \,\}$$

The production function only selects efficient points from the input requirement set. The concept of production function was introduced earlier in Chapter 3.

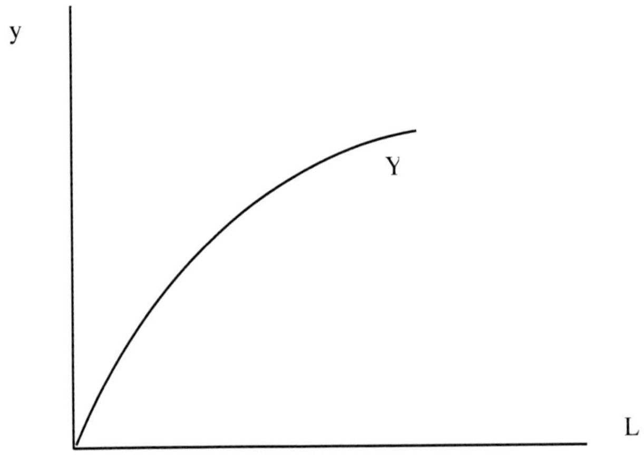

Figure 4.1

We now introduce the well known Cobb-Douglas production function. With the help of this function we will introduce these concepts. A Cobb-Douglas production function is given below:

$$y = V_1^{\alpha} V_2^{\beta} \qquad \alpha + \beta = 1$$

We can now define:

Production plan: $Y = \{(y, -V_1, -V_2) : y \le V_1^{\alpha} V_2^{\beta}\}$

IRS: $G(y^*) = \{(V_1, V_2) : y^* \le V_1^{\alpha} V_2^{\beta}\}$

Isoquant: $Q(y^*) = \{(V_1, V_2) : y^* = V_1^{\alpha} V_2^{\beta}\}$

We can now draw an isoquant for the above technology.

Recall that in consumer theory we had introduced indifference curves. The counter part of these in production theory are the isoquants. Notice the marked region shows the input requirement set and is analogous to the better than or as good as set in consumption theory. The most commonly used production functions are given below:

Constant Elasticity of Substitution (CES):

$$f(V_1, V_2) = \left[V_1^{\rho} + V_2^{\rho}\right]^{1/\rho}$$

Generalized Cobb Douglas:

$$f(V_1, V_2) = V_1^{\alpha} V_2^{\beta}$$

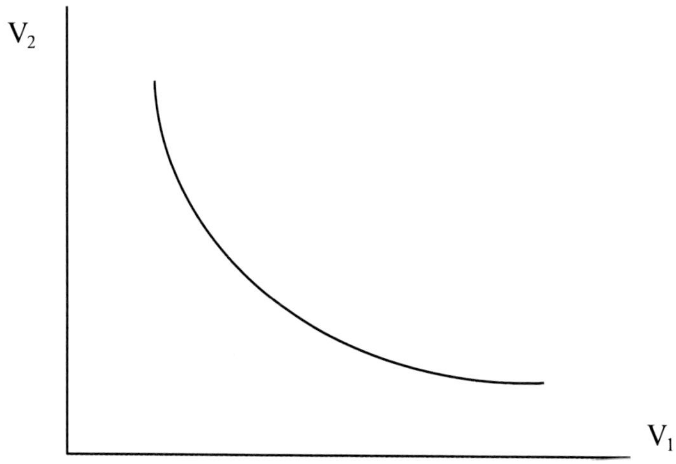

Figure 4.2

Leontief production function:

$$f(V_1, V_2) = \min[aV_1, bV_2]$$

Figure 4.3 shows the isoquant for the Leontief technology. It should be noted that both the Cobb-Douglas and Leontief production functions are a subset of the CES function.

Recall that in consumer theory we placed a lot of emphasis on convexity. In fact in most of economics convexity is a very important and desirable property. In general it is assumed that the input requirement set is convex. Formally, we can write this as:

Convexity: If the input vectors V and V' belong to *G(y)* then $\lambda v + (1-\lambda)V'$ for $0 \leq \lambda \leq 1$ also belong to *G(y)*.

In consumer theory we had defined the concept of marginal rate of substitution. We can now do the same in production theory. We assume that the production function is twice differentiable. Then it follows that:

$$y = f[V_1, V_2]$$

Differentiating this totally gives us:

$$dy = \frac{\partial f}{\partial V_1} dV_1 + \frac{\partial f}{\partial V_2} dV_2$$

Leontief isoquant

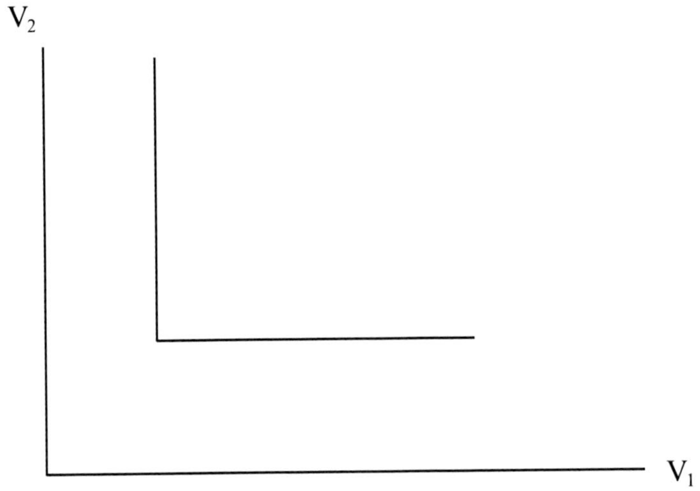

Figure 4.3

On an isoquant there is no movement in output as all points on it give rise to same level of output so *y=0* and it follows that:

$$\frac{dV_2}{dV_1} = -\frac{\partial f / \partial V_1}{\partial f / \partial V_2}$$

This is known as the technical rate of substitution.

Recall that we had defined elasticity as logarithm differentiation of the ratio of two variables:

$$\varepsilon = \frac{d \log y}{d \log x} = \frac{y}{x} \frac{dy}{dx}$$

Let us now define the elasticity of substitution which is the elasticity at a particular point of an isoquant:

$$\sigma = \frac{\frac{d(V_2/V_1)}{V_2/V_1}}{\frac{d(TRS)}{TRS}} = \frac{TRS}{\frac{V_2}{V_1}} \frac{d\left(\frac{V_2}{V_1}\right)}{d(TRS)}$$

Let us take the Cobb-Douglas case:

$$y = V_1^{\alpha} V_2^{\beta}$$

$$\frac{\partial y}{\partial V_1} = \alpha V_1^{\alpha-1} V_2^{\beta}$$

$$\frac{\partial y}{\partial V_2} = \beta V_1^{\alpha} V_2^{\beta-1}$$

$$\frac{dV_2}{dV_1} = TRS = -\frac{\alpha V_1^{\alpha-1} V_2^{\beta}}{\beta V_1^{\alpha} V_2^{\beta-1}} = -\frac{\alpha}{\beta} \frac{V_2}{V_1}$$

It follows that:

$$\frac{V_2}{V_1} = -\frac{\beta}{\alpha} TRS$$

By taking logs and absolute value we obtain:

$$\log\left(\frac{V_2}{V_1}\right) = \log\left(\frac{\beta}{\alpha}\right) + \log TRS$$

$$\sigma = \frac{d\log\left(\frac{V_2}{V_1}\right)}{d\log(TRS)} = 1$$

This technique can be used to obtain the elasticities of various production functions.

Inputs can be increased proportionately or non-proportionately. Returns to scale are defined in terms of varying all inputs in the same proportion. Return to factors are defined for non-proportionate change (the extreme case being when only one factor is allowed to vary and all other factors are held constant).

Constant Returns to Scale (CRS): A production function exhibits constant returns to scale when:

$$y = f[\lambda V_1, \lambda V_2, \ldots \lambda V_n] = \lambda f[\ldots]$$

provided that $\lambda > 0$.

Increasing Returns to Scale (IRS):
A production function exhibits increasing returns to scale when:

$$f[\lambda V_1, \lambda V_2, ... \lambda V_n] > \lambda f[V_1, V_2, ... V_n]$$

for any $\lambda > 1$ and $[......] > 0$.

Decreasing Returns to Scale (DRS):
A production function exhibits decreasing returns to scale when:

$$f[\lambda V_1, \lambda V_2, ... \lambda V_N] < \lambda f[V_1, ... V_N]$$

for any $\lambda > 1$ and $[......] > 0$.

Homogeneity: A production function $F : R_+^n \rightarrow R$ is homogenous of degree n if and only if $f[\lambda V_1, ... \lambda V_n] = \lambda^n f[V_1 ... V_n]$ for any $\lambda > 1$ and $V \in R_+^n$.

Profit Maximization:
We will now extend our analysis to the n input case and consider the 2×1 case as a subset. Let p be the price of output y and $V = [V_1, V_2, ..., V_n]$ a vector of inputs. Then the firm chooses (y,-V) to maximize:

$$py - w_1 V_1 - w_2 V_2 - ... - w_n V_n$$

Subject to :

$$(y, -V) \in Y$$

By substituting the production function of y we obtain:

$$pf[V_1, V_2, ..., V_n] - w_1 V_1 - w_2 V_2 - ... - w_n V_n$$

By differentiating this with respect to V_i holding p and $w_i (i = 1..n)$ constant we obtain:

$$p \frac{\partial f}{\partial V_1} - w_1 = 0$$

$$\cdots$$

$$p \frac{\partial f}{\partial V_n} - w_n = 0$$

These conditions state that for an interior solution the value of the marginal product of a factor must equal its reward. The second order conditions for profit maximization require that

$$H = \begin{bmatrix} pf_{11} \cdots pf_{1n} \\ \cdots \\ pf_{n1} \cdots pf_{nn} \end{bmatrix}$$

is negative definite.

If f is concave then the first order conditions are sufficient for a maximum for the profit function. From the above system we obtain n unconditional input demand functions:

$$\begin{aligned} V_1 &= V_1[p, w_1, \ldots, w_n] \\ V_2 &= V_2[p, w_1, \ldots, w_n] \\ &\cdots \\ V_n &= V_n[p, w_1, \ldots, w_n] \end{aligned}$$

The supply function is obtained by substituting the V_i's in the production function.

$$y[p, w_1, \ldots, w_n] = f[V_1(\ldots), V_2(\ldots), \ldots, V_n(\ldots)] = f(p, w)$$

Note that factor demand and supply function are homogeneous of degree zero in (p, w).

The properties of the profit function are intuitively obvious. They are similar to the indirect utility function in demand theory. These are:

1. Profit function is non-decreasing in commodity price and non-increasing in input prices.
2. The profit function is homogenous of degree 1 in all prices both commodity and factor.
3. The profit function is convex in commodity price and input price.
4. Profit function is continuous.

Proofs are similar to those given for the indirect utility function.

Recall that we obtained the profit function by changing it from the quantity into price space. This is achieved by expressing the output and input in terms of commodity and factor price so the profit function is expressed as:

$$\pi = \pi[p, w_1, \ldots, w_n]$$

We can now apply the Envelope theorem to obtain the supply and input demand functions. This is known as the Hotellings Lemma.

$$\frac{\partial \pi}{\partial p} = y(p, w) \qquad \text{Supply function}$$

$$\frac{\partial \pi}{\partial w_i} = -V_i(p, w) \quad i = 1, \ldots, n \qquad \text{the unconditional input demand functions}$$

Recall in consumer theory we wrote the duality of the consumers' utility maximization problem in terms of the expenditure minimization problem. We can do exactly the same in the theory of the firm. We can write the cost minimization problem as:

Minimize: $w_1 V_1 + w_2 V_2 + \ldots + w_n V_n$

Subject to

$$\bar{y} = f[V_1, V_2, \ldots, V_n]$$

Where $\bar{y}$ denotes a fixed level of output. The solution to the first order conditions of the above problem gives us the conditional input demand functions:

$$V_1 = V_1[\bar{y}, w_1, \ldots, w_n]$$
$$V_2 = V_2[\bar{y}, w_1, \ldots, w_n]$$
$$V_n = V_n[\bar{y}, w_1, \ldots, w_n]$$

The cost function is obtained by substituting the conditional input demand functions into the cost function-again to convert it into the price and output space:

$$c = c[\bar{y}, w_1, \ldots, w_n]$$

The properties of the cost function are:

i. Cost function is non-decreasing in $w_1, \ldots, w_n$.
ii. Cost function is homogenous of degree 1 in input prices.
iii. Cost function is concave in $w_1, \ldots, w_n$.
iv. Cost function is continuous in $w_1, \ldots, w_n$.

Proofs – same as for the expenditure function.
Shepherd's Lemma can be utilized for obtaining the input demand functions:

$$\frac{\partial c[\bar{y}, w_1, \ldots, w_n]}{\partial w_1} = V_1[\bar{y}, w_1, \ldots, w_n]$$

$$\ldots$$

$$\frac{\partial c[\bar{y}, w_1, \ldots, w_n]}{\partial w_n} = V_n[\bar{y}, w_1, \ldots, w_n]$$

These are known as the conditional input demand functions. They are analogous to the compensated demand curves in consumption theory.

By concavity:

$$\frac{\partial V_i\left[\bar{y}, w_1, \ldots, w_n\right]}{\partial w_i} < 0 \qquad (i = 1 \ldots n)$$

So the conditional input demand functions are well behaved.

Note that marginal cost can be obtained by differentiating the cost function with respect to output.

$$\frac{\partial c}{\partial \bar{y}} = \text{Marginal Cost} = \text{MC}$$

It is now trivial to prove that in the competitive case price equals marginal cost for a firm.

$$\text{Profit} = \pi = py - c(y)$$

$$\therefore \frac{\partial \pi}{\partial y} = p - c'(y) = 0$$

$$p = c'(y)$$

Price = Marginal Cost at the point of competitive equilibrium.

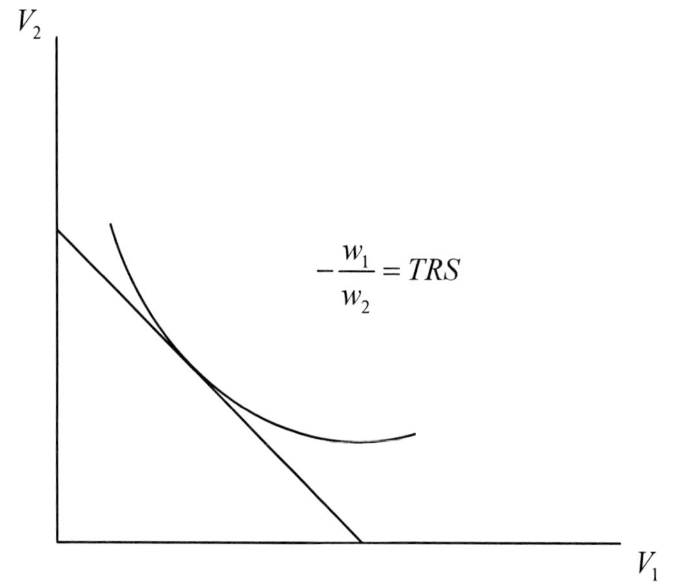

Figure 4.4

In our discussion so far we have assumed that all factors are variable. This is defined as long run. A short run situation is defined as one in which some factors of production are fixed, that is, their level is already known to us. Recall that we denoted the vector of inputs as $V = (V_1, V_2, ... V_n)$. We can split this up into V_f and V_v where they denote fixed and variable factors respectively. We can now rewrite our cost function as:

$$c(w, y, V_f) = w_v V_v(w, y, V_f) + w_f V_f$$

where: $$w = (w_1, w_2, ... w_n)$$

$$V_v = (V_1, V_2, ... V_j)$$
$$V_f = (V_{j+1}, ... V_n)$$

Now the costs have been split into two parts variable costs as denoted by $w_v V_v$ and fixed costs $w_f V_f$. The following concepts can now be defined:

Long run total cost $= w_1 V_1 + w_2 V_2 + w_n V_n$

$= wV$

Long run marginal cost

$$= \frac{\partial c[w, y, V]}{\partial y}$$ already shown

Long run average cost

$$= \frac{c[w, y, V]}{y}$$

Short run average cost

$$= \frac{c(w, y, V_f)}{y}$$

Short run average variable cost

$$= \frac{w_v V_v}{y}$$

Short run average fixed cost

$$= \frac{w_f V_f}{y}$$

Short run marginal cost

$$= \frac{\partial c(w, y, V_f)}{\partial y}$$

Note that the long run cost function can be written as:

$$c[w, y] = c(w, y, V_f[w, y])$$

This function can be used to define long run average and marginal cost.

It is extremely easy to solve for the various concepts in the two factor one output case. It is left to the reader to do the short run case. It is also straight forward to do the geometry of cost curves.

Recall that in discussing consumption theory we examined several concepts related to duality. The same can be done in production theory. The ideas are presented below in tabular form:

Consumption Theory	Production Theory
Utility function $U = U(X_1, X_2)$	Production function $y = f(V_1, V_2)$
Indifference curve $\overline{U} = U(X_1, X_2)$	Isoquant $\overline{y} = f(V_1, V_2)$
Indirect indifference curve $V = V[\overline{P}_1, \overline{P}_2]$	Indirect isoquant $\overline{c} = g(w_1, w_2)$

The isoquant and isoprice (isocost) indirect isoquants are shown in Figure 4.5.

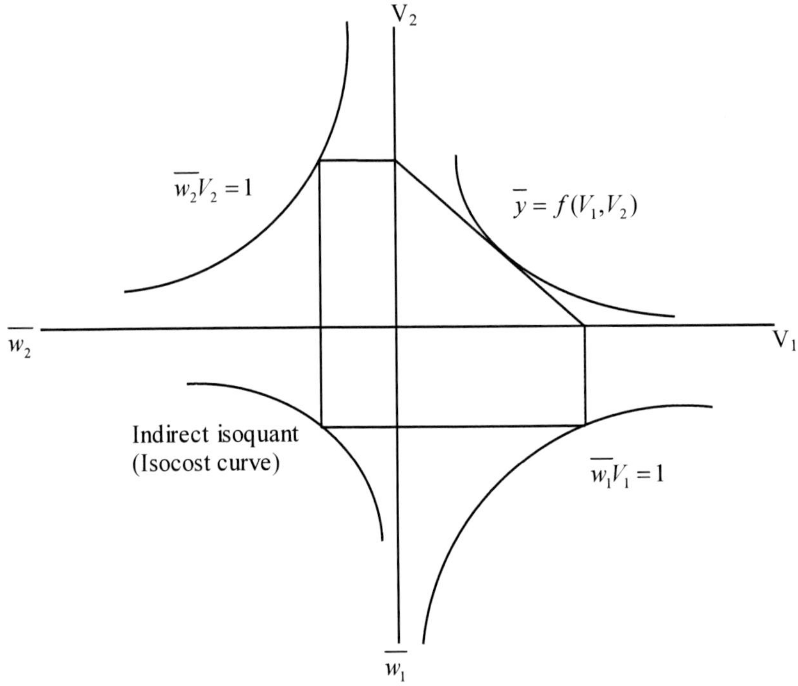

Figure 4.5

A Cobb-Douglas function provides an easy way of showing duality relations. We know that:

Cobb-Douglas production function $y = V_1^{\alpha} V_2^{1-\alpha}$

The cost function for this technology is given by:

$$c[w_1, w_2, \overline{y}] = \overline{y} w_1^{\alpha} w_2^{1-\alpha}$$

By using Shephard's theorem:

$$V_1[w_1, w_2, \overline{y}] = \alpha \overline{y} \left[\frac{w_2}{w_1} \right]^{1-\alpha}$$

This is increasing in $\overline{y}, w_2$ and falling in w_1.

$$V_2[w_1, w_2, \overline{y}] = (1-\alpha) \overline{y} \left[\frac{w_2}{w_1} \right]^{-\alpha}$$

Similarly this is increasing in $\overline{y}, w_1$ and falling in w_2 by rearranging we obtain:

$$\frac{w_2}{w_1} = \left(\frac{V_1}{\alpha \bar{y}} \right)^{\frac{1}{1-\alpha}}$$

$$\frac{w_2}{w_1} = \left(\frac{V_2}{\alpha \bar{y}} \right)^{-\frac{1}{\alpha}}$$

We know that:

$$\left(\frac{V_1}{\alpha \bar{y}} \right)^{\frac{1}{1-\alpha}} = \left(\frac{V_2}{\alpha \bar{y}} \right)^{-\frac{1}{\alpha}}$$

It follows:

$$\frac{V_1^{-\alpha}}{\alpha^{-\alpha} \bar{y}^{-\alpha}} = \frac{V_2^{-\alpha}}{(1-\alpha)^{1-\alpha} \bar{y}^{1-\alpha}}$$

or

$$y = V_1^{\alpha} V_2^{1-\alpha}$$

Thus duality works beautifully for the Cobb Douglas production function. Figure 4.5 is drawn using the same technique as in consumption theory.

Chapter 5

EXCHANGE AND THE TWO FUNDAMENTAL THEOREMS OF WELFARE ECONOMICS

We have spent a lot of time analyzing the behaviour of individual agents: a consumer who maximizes utility subject to a given budget constraint and a producer who maximizes profit subject to a technology constraint. Using these concepts we also analyzed the functions of markets, for example, price determination in competitive markets.

It is appropriate now to move on and analyze interaction among various economic agents and determine prices, outputs and trade endogenously. This is known as general equilibrium. These models can be very simple like the Heckscher Ohlin model of trade or like the Arrow-Debreu-Hahn models of full fledged general equilibrium. In these models three important questions are generally raised. First: Does a solution exist? Second: Is the solution unique? Finally: Is the solution stable? The mathematical tools used for these purposes become quite difficult and require some knowledge of analysis and topology. The theorems most often used belong to the class of fixed point theorems. Most often the Brouwer's fixed point theorem is used – a theorem that looks very simple in the two dimensional space but is quite difficult to prove and understand in higher dimensions.

To develop an insight into the operation of these models we begin by analyzing an exchange economy in which there is no production. On the basis of this model we will present the two fundamental theorems of welfare economics. The first theorem states that any competitive equilibrium is Pareto Optimal. The second theorem (a converse of the first) states that any Pareto Optimal state can be decentralized as a competitive equilibrium with transfer payments. As we proceed we shall explain some of the above terms.

Let us begin by defining a good. This was done rigorously by Debreu in his classic monograph. A commodity is defined by three characteristics: (i) time (ii) location and (iii) the state of the world. Drinking a latte in Hong Kong is not the same as drinking it in front of Notre Dame. We will assume that a market exists for each good.

In exchange models only consumers are present and there is no production. So our economic agents are consumers indexed from $i=1 \ldots n$. For graphical purposes we shall reduce them to $i=1,2$. Think of primary school children who bring lunch boxes to school. They are not producers and the food in the lunch boxes represents their endowment. Primary school children often exchange food. This exchange can be given a very rigorous theme. Two themes are involved in this process:

Theme One: [Edgeworth]: Individual consumers (for example, school children) may be able to improve their welfare by exchanging goods (that is redistribution).

Theme Two: (Walras): Prices and markets would allow individuals to reach their most preferred bundle without the need for cooperating with each other. We now proceed to develop these ideas.

We shall assume that each individual has a utility function (hence, all the individuals have an ordering which we discussed earlier in these lectures). So we have n utility functions U_1, U_2, U_j, U_n. Note that the subscripts denote individuals. Suppose that there are ℓ commodities and they run from $1 \ldots \ell$. Each individual has an endowment of each of these commodities which is assumed to be non-negative. This information can be expressed in the following form:

$$U_1 = V_1\left[X_1^1, X_1^2 \ldots X_1^\ell\right]$$

$$U_2 = V_2\left[X_2^1, X_2^2 \ldots X_2^\ell\right]$$

$$U_n = V_n\left[X_n^1, X_n^2 \ldots X_n^\ell\right]$$

Note that superscripts denote commodities and subscripts denote individuals.

The endowments are given by:

$$E^1 = \sum_{i=1}^{n} E_i^1$$

which is the total endowment of good 1,

$$E^2 = \sum_{i=1}^{n} E_i^2$$

and so on.

Each individual maximizes utility subject to an endowment constraint, therefore:

$$Max\, U_1\left[X_1^1, X_1^2, \ldots X_1^\ell\right]$$

subject to:

$$P_1 X_1^1 + P_2 X_1^2 + P_\ell X_1^\ell = P_1 E_1^1 + P_2 E_1^2 + P_\ell E_1^\ell$$

This process provides an optimal consumption bundle as a function of prices and endowment. Let the bundles be denoted by:

$$X_1 = \left(x_1^1, x_1^2 \ldots x_1^\ell\right)$$

$$X_n = \left(x_n^1, x_n^2 \ldots x_n^\ell\right)$$

Now we can define an economy wide allocation which will be:

$$X = \left(x_1^1 + x_2^1 + \ldots x_n^1, x_1^2 + x_2^2 + \ldots x_n^2, \ldots\right)$$

Finally feasibility of the system requires that:

$$x_1^1 + x_2^1 + \ldots + x_n^1 = E_1^1 + E_2^1 + E_n^1 = E^1$$

and so on.

To obtain insight into the whole process let us reduce this to a problem in two dimension space. We know that:

$$E^1 = E_1^1 + E_2^1$$

and

$$E^2 = E_1^2 + E_2^2$$

So we can construct a box of the dimension E^1 and E^2 as the total endowment is given exogenously. Consider two individuals: d_U and d_i. Suppose that d_U has 10 English sandwiches in her lunch box. Let d_i have six mars bars. Therefore:

$$E^S = 10 + 0 = 10$$

$$E^M = 0 + 6 = 6$$

The dimension of the Edgeworth box then is 10 and 6 as drawn in Figure 5.1.

The total amount of commodity 1 is represented by the two horizontal axes and of good 2 by the two vertical axes. $d_U d_U$'s origin is in the left hand corner of the box and $d_i d_i$'s origin is in the top right hand corner of the box. The way we have chosen the endowment the right hand corner denotes the endowment for the whole economy. Note that any point in this box represents a feasible allocation between the two individuals. We can now plot the strictly convex to the origin indifference curves for d_U and d_i as shown in Figure 5.1. Having represented this information we have to work out an equilibrium position for d_U and d_i such that the Edgeworth and Walras themes can be represented.

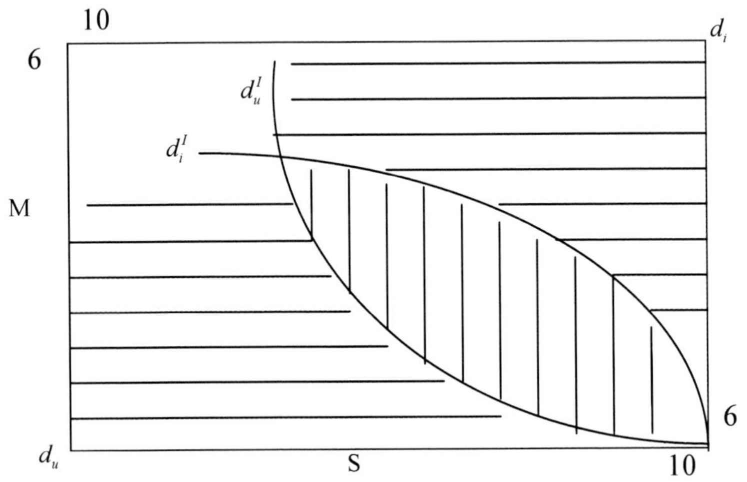

Figure 5.1

The two indifference curves which pass through the endowment point divide the box in three areas. An area of intersection denoted by straight lines including the boundary and areas depicted by straight lines. At this stage let us introduce Pareto rule (also known as Pareto Criteria). This can be stated in the following ways:

i. If all individuals in the society are indifferent between two social states *x* and *y* (*xIy* for all *i*) then society should also be indifferent between *x* and *y*.

ii. If at least one individual in the society strictly prefers *x* to *y* (*xPy* for some *i*) and every other member of the society regards *x* to be at least as good as *y* then the society should prefer *x* to *y*.

Using the Pareto Criteria (sometimes referred to as Pareto rule) the area of interest for us is the region with straight lines. These represent allocations that can either improve the welfare of both d_U and d_i or of at least one of them leaving the welfare of the other individual at the same level as that given by the endowment point. This lens shaped area is defined as the core of an economy.

CORE: In an exchange economy this represents that set of allocations that can not be improved by any coalition of individuals.

In the example given the core is not empty. One can construct examples of an empty core. Consider a society consisting of two individuals: (i) Hindu (H) and (ii) a Muslim (M). Both are assumed to be believers. Now consider an exchange economy that consists of two goods: beef and pork. Hindu does not eat beef and the Muslim does not eat pork. We assume the absence of externalities so that at least they are tolerant of each other and do not resent the fact that the other party consumes the prohibited meat. Their preferences are represented in Figure 5.2. In this particular case the core is empty and the themes of Edgeworth and Walras do not apply.

WALRASIAN EQUILIBRIUM

Let us take an arbitrary price vector $P = [P_1, P_2]$. We assume that at the initial stage the prices are given from outside. It does not imply that this is a market clearing price. So the maximization problem of the consumer is:

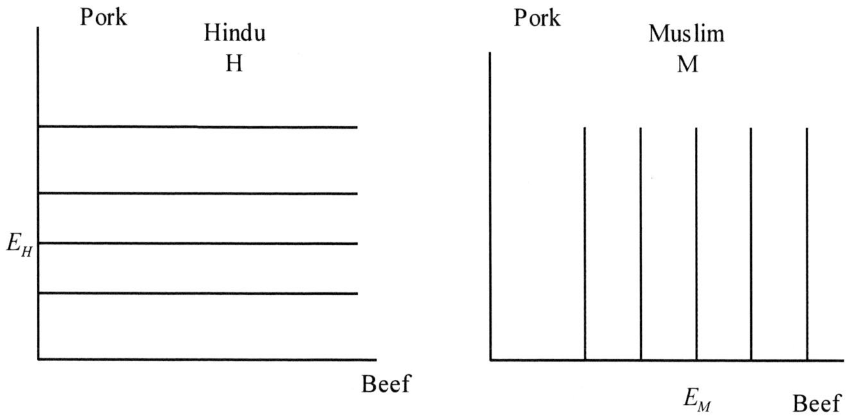

Figure 5.2

Maximize $U[X_1^1, X_1^2]$

Sub to $\quad P_1X_1^1 + P_2X_1^2 = P_1E_1^1 + P_2E_1^2$

From the maximization exercise we obtain two demand functions for individual 1:

$$X_1^1 = X_1^1[P_1, P_2, P_1E_1^1 + P_2E_1^2]$$
$$X_1^2 = X_1^2[P_1, P_2, P_1E_2^1 + P_2E_2^2]$$

Similarly for the second individual.

Let us take the Cobb Douglas Case for d_U and d_i.

$$U_V = \left(X_{d_U}^1\right)^{1/2}\left(X_{d_U}^2\right)^{1/2}$$

sub to $\quad P_1X_{d_U}^1 + P_2X_{d_U}^2 = P_1(10)$

The maximization gives us the following demand functions:

$$X_{d_U}^1 = \frac{10}{2} = 5$$

$$X_{d_U}^2 = \frac{P_1}{P_2}5$$

Let the utility function for $d_{in}d_{in}$ be given by:

$$V_{d_i} = \left(X^1_{d_i}\right)^{1/3}\left(X^2_{d_i}\right)^{2/3}$$

and the budget constraint

$$P_1 X^1_{d_i} + P_2 X^2_{d_i} = P_2(6)$$

solving this maximization problem we obtain:

$$X^1_{d_i} = \frac{P_2}{P_1}(6)$$

$$X^2_{d_i} = 4$$

We now define a Walrasian equilibrium. This refers to a baris.

$$\left(P_1^*, P_2^*, \left(X_1^1, X_1^2\right)^*, \left(X_2^1, X_2^2\right)^*\right)$$

such that:

$$X_1^1 + X_2^1 \leq E_1^1 + E_2^1$$

and

$$X_1^2 + X_2^2 \leq E_2^1 + E_2^2$$

or

$$\left(X_1^2 - E_2^1\right) + \left(X_2^2 - E_2^2\right) \leq 0$$

Note that $\left(X_1^1 - E_1^1\right)$ defines the excess demand for good 1 and so on. The definition given above is known as the weak definition of the Walrasian equilibrium. It shows that excess demand cannot be positive. It is either zero or negative. Figure 5.3 shows a typical excess demand function. Note that the Walrasian definition confines solution only to the left hand side of the lower part of Figure 5.3.

We can denote the excess demand functions as:

$$Z^1\left[P_1, P_2\right] = \left[X_1^1 + X_1^2 - \left(E_1^1 + E_2^1\right)\right]$$

$$Z^2\left[P_1, P_2\right] = \left[X_1^2 + X_2^2 - \left(E_1^2 + E_2^2\right)\right]$$

These are also homogenous of degree zero in prices.

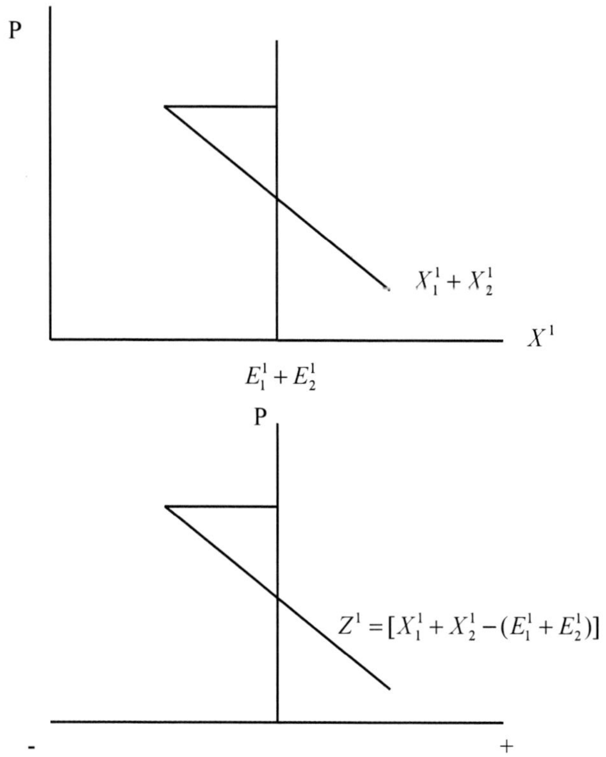

Figure 5.3

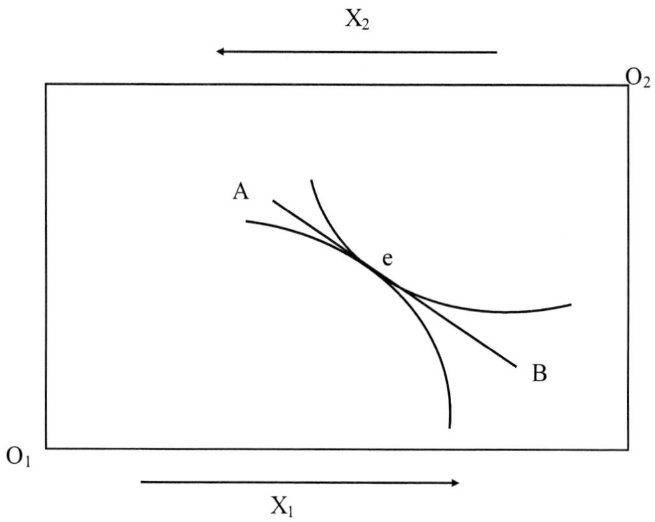

Figure 5.4

Given the above definition the Walrasian equilibrium is shown geometrically in Figure 5.4. The slope of line *AB* is the competitive price ratio and point *E* the endowment point. What do we notice about point *e*? Position *e* represents a point of competitive equilibrium which is also Pareto Optimal. This requires two characteristics:

1. Each consumer is maximizing utility subject to a budget constraint.
2. Excess demand is equal to zero.

Now it is clear that any departure from point *e* would represent a decline in the welfare of one of the individuals. Therefore, point *e* represents a position of Pareto Optimality. Since excess demand equals zero and both consumers are maximizing utility it is a point of competitive equilibrium which is Pareto Optimal. For our example:

$$5+\frac{P_2}{P_1}6=10$$

Therefore the equilibrium price ratio is:

$$\left(\frac{P_2}{P_1}\right)=5/6$$

It is easily verified that:

$$5+\frac{5}{6}(6)=10$$

and the markets clear and are Pareto Optimal. In calculus terms this implies that $MRS_{d_U} = MRS_{d_i}$.

While it is very nice to draw graphs and illustrations they do not provide proofs. So we have to prove that a Walrasian equilibrium exists. For this we have to use the famous Brouwer fixed point theorem. Let us work our way through this proof. Let us first state the Brouwer Fixed point theorem:

If $f: S_n \to S_n$ then there exists an $\overline{x} \in S_n$ such that $f(\overline{x}) = \overline{x}$. The term $\overline{x}$ is a fixed point for the function $f(\cdot)$.

We provide a widely used graph to illustrate this theorem. This graph is available in many text books on microeconomics. We express the theorem in two dimensional space:

Let f be a mapping from the closed interval [0,1] to the closed interval [0,1] or $f[0,1] \to [0,1]$. Let this be a continuous function, then there exists a fixed point $\overline{x}$ which belongs to [0,1] such that $f(\overline{x}) = \overline{x}$.

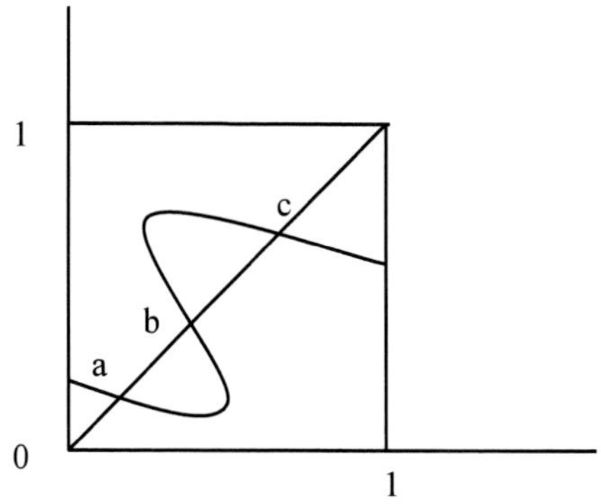

Figure 5.5

Proof: consider the following:

If $f(0)=0$ then this is a fixed point.
If $f(1)=1$ then this is also a fixed point.

Now consider the case such that $f(0)\neq 0$ and $f(1)\neq 1$. In this case we define the following function:

$$G(x)=f(x)-x$$

We have to show that at $x=\bar{x}$ $G(x)=0$ then $f(\bar{x})=\bar{x}$, which is the fixed point.

$$G(0)=f(0)-0=f(0)>0$$
$$G(1)=f(1)-1<0$$

Hence $G:[0,1]\rightarrow R G(0)G(1)<0$. We know that $f(x)$ is continuous therefore $G(0,1)\rightarrow R$ is also continuous. Hence, by Intermediate Value Theorem there exists an $\bar{x}\in[0,1]$ such that $G(\bar{x})=0$, hence, $f(\bar{x})=\bar{x}$.

Proof in the two dimensional case:

$$\begin{aligned}(p_1,p_2)(z^1,z^2)=\ & p_1X_1^1+p_1X_2^1-p_1e_1^1-p_1e_2^1\\ & +p_2X_1^2+p_2X_2^2-p_2e_1^2-p_2e_2^2\end{aligned}$$

For each individual

$$p_1X_1^1+p_2X_1^2=p_1e_1^1+p_2e_1^2$$

and

$$p_1X_2^1 + p_2X_2^2 = p_1e_2^1 + p_2e_2^2$$

Hence

$$(p_1, p_2)(z^1, z^2) = 0$$

It also follows trivially from Walras' law that we only have to clear k-1 markets. Hence, in the two good case if one market is in equilibrium so will be the other market. This is the reason for working with only one market in general equilibrium models which have two markets.

Let us now define free goods. If p^* is a Walrasian equilibrium and $z_j(p^*) < 0$ then $p^* = 0$. (Varian). This is illustrated in Figure 5.6.

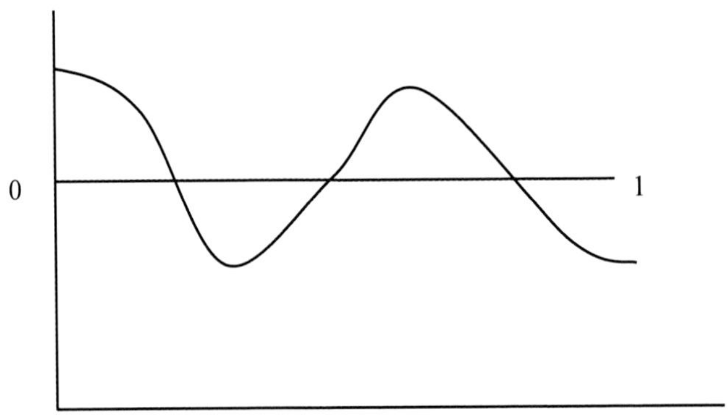

Figure 5.6

We have to convert the two dimensional problem into a framework in which we can apply the Brouwer fixed point theorem. First, we normalize prices.

$$\hat{P}_1 = \frac{P_1}{P_1 + P_2}$$

$$\hat{P}_2 = \frac{P_2}{P_1 + P_2}$$

Therefore:

$$\hat{P}_1 + \hat{P}_2 = 1$$

So we have defined a unit simplex in the two dimensional case.

We know the following: If $\left(Z^1, Z^2\right): S \to R^2$ is a continuous function that satisfies Walras' law that is $\left(P_1, P_2\right)\left(Z^1, Z^2\right) = 0$ then there exists a $\hat{P}^* \in S$ such that $\left(Z^1, Z^2\right) \leq 0$.

We know that:

$$\begin{aligned}(p_1, p_2)\left(z^1, z^2\right) = p_1 X_1^1 + p_2 X_2^1 - p_1 e_1^1 - p_2 e_2^1 \\ + p_2 X_1^2 + p_2 X_2^2 - p_2 e_1^2 - p_2 e_2^2\end{aligned}$$

Now each individual maximizes utility, therefore, it follows that:

$$p_1 X_1^1 + p_2 X_1^2 = p_1 e_1^1 + p_2 e_1^2$$

and

$$p_1 X_2^1 + p_2 X_2^2 = p_1 e_2^1 + p_2 e_2^2$$

therefore

$$(p_1, p_2)\left(z^1, z^2\right) = 0$$

Following Varian we construct a mapping g:

Proof:

$$g_1\left[\frac{P_1}{P_1 + P_2}, \frac{P_2}{P_1 + P_2}\right] = g\left[\hat{P}_1, \hat{P}_2\right]$$

$$= \frac{\hat{P}_1 + \max\left[0, z^1\left(\frac{P_1}{P_1 + P_2}, \frac{P_2}{P_1 + P_2}\right)\right]}{1 + \max\left[0, z^1\left(\frac{P_1}{P_1 + P_2}, \frac{P_2}{P_1 + P_2}\right)\right] + \max\left[0, z^2\left(\frac{P_1}{P_1 + P_2}, \frac{P_2}{P_1 + P_2}\right)\right]}$$

Now $g_1 + g_2 = 1$ and z^i the excess demand functions are continuous. Therefore, the conditions for the Brouwer's fixed point theorem are satisfied. Therefore, there exists a $\hat{P}^*$ such that:

$$\hat{P}^* = g\left(\hat{P}^*\right)$$

$$\hat{P}^* = g_1\left[\frac{P_1}{P_1 + P_2}, \frac{P_2}{P_1 + P_2}\right] = \frac{\hat{P}_1^* + \max\left[0, z^1\right]}{1 + \max\left(0, z^1\right) + \max\left(0, z^2\right)}$$

It follows that:

$$\hat{P}^*\left[1+\max\left(0,z^1\right)+\max\left(0,z^2\right)\right]=\hat{P}_1^*+\max\left(0,z^1\right)$$

therefore:

$$\hat{P}^*\max\left(0,z^1\right)+\hat{P}^*\max\left(0,z^2\right)=\max\left(0,z^1\right)$$

By a similar procedure and adding we obtain:

$$\hat{P}_1 z^1\left[\max\left(0,z^1\right)+\max\left(0,z^2\right)\right]+\hat{P}_2 z^2\left[\max\left(0,z^1\right)+\max\left(0,z^2\right)\right]$$
$$=z^1\max\left(0,z^1\right)+z^2\max\left(0,z^2\right)$$

By Walras' law the left hand side goes to zero.

$$z^1\max\left(0,z^1\right)+z^2\max\left(0,z^2\right)=0$$

Now each term is either greater than or equal to zero. So if both terms are zero then we have an equilibrium. If no then we have a contradiction as the equality would not hold.

The major beauty of this result is that equilibrium can be reached without the assistance from a central planner. Primary School children do exchange goods from their lunch boxes and establish without realizing it that mutual cooperation is welfare improving and there exists a competitive equilibrium with prices at which they maximize utility.

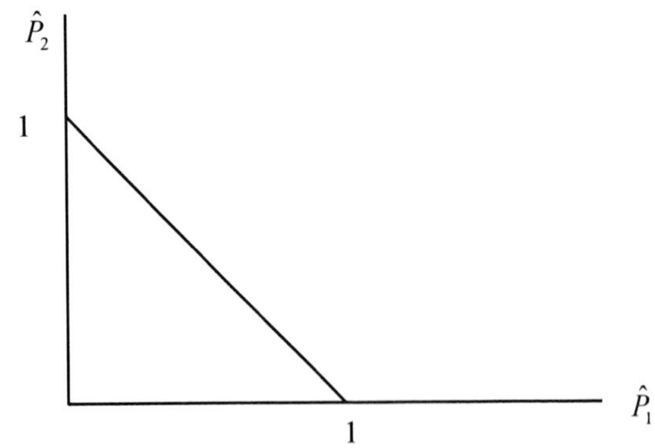

Figure 5.7

Now we consider the theorem that a Pareto efficient (Pareto Optimal) allocation can be decentralized as a competitive equilibrium with appropriate transfer payments. This is an extremely important result as a Pareto Optimal position may look very ugly or unsatisfactory from certain ethical judgments. Consider Figure 5.7. In this diagram point *e* is Pareto Optimal with the rich having lots of both goods and the poor very little of both goods. The second theorem tells us that we can choose a Pareto Optimal point then there exists a transfer payment and a set of prices that will make that point a competitive equilibrium. Varian's proof of this is very simple using the revealed preference approach. We suggest you read the book for the proof of this result.

These theorems provide some very important policy guidelines. The price system in the absence of distortions allows an economy to reach a Pareto Optimal where all gains from trade are captured. If there is no price distortion then this process is automatic. The second theorem shows that equitable allocations can be achieved by transfer payments. Therefore, the message is loud and clear do not distort markets.

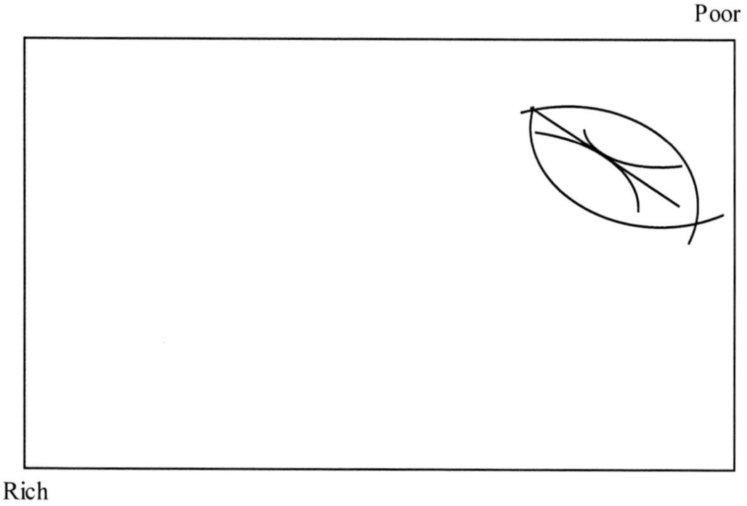

Figure 5.8

Chapter 6

GENERAL EQUILIBRIUM: A SIMPLE TREATMENT VIA THE TWO-SECTOR MODEL OF GENERAL EQUILIBRIUM

On the basis of an exchange economy we established two fundamental theorems of economics. We established that every competitive equilibrium is Pareto Optimal. And we also established that every Pareto Optimum position can be made to correspond to a competitive equilibrium. The importance of the second theorem arises from the fact that while a competitive equilibrium is efficient it may not represent an allocation that is satisfactory from the point of view of income distribution. The second welfare theorem addresses this issue. It requires choosing the income of agents in such a way that the Pareto Optimal allocation can be realized as a decentralized allocation via the price mechanism. As stated earlier it requires making lump sum transfers. We now move on and establish these results in a model with production.

Students find general equilibrium very hard to understand. Of course, there are many models of general equilibrium which require that many agents interact with each other. The simplest way to accomplish this is to teach the two sector model of general equilibrium which is widely used in trade and also growth theory. The model is a cornerstone of the Heckscher-Ohlin, the Ricardo-Samuelson-Viner-Jones, the Harris-Todaro and many other models that are widely used in trade and development literature. There is also a large body of literature on two-sector growth theory both in the Solow and endogenous growth theory framework.

A TWO-SECTOR MODEL OF AN ECONOMY

We consider an economy that produces two commodities, X_1 and X_2. The aggregate utility function for the country as a whole is given by :

$$U = U(X_1, X_2) \tag{6.1}$$

where U indicates total utility and $X_i(i=1,2)$ the consumption of commodity $Y_i(i=1,2)$. The utility function is assumed to be strictly concave and $U_i = \partial U / \partial X_i$, the marginal utility of consuming good i is assumed to be positive. It will suffice to assume that the utility function is quasi-concave but for geometrical reasons the assumption of strict concavity will generally be maintained. The aggregate utility function is assumed to possess both behavioural and welfare significance.

Given utility maximization and a position of interior equilibrium for the representative agent, if follows that:

$$\frac{U_2}{U_1} = \frac{P_2}{P_1} = P \tag{6.2}$$

where U_i and P_i ($i = 1,2$) denote the marginal utility and the ith price, respectively. In small open economies the terms of trade, P, are given exogenously. However, in a closed economy the relative price is determined endogenously. This condition shows that, in a position of utility maximizing equilibrium, the domestic rate of substitution in consumption equals the ratio of commodity prices and is the national counterpart of the condition of individual maximization in the theory of consumer behaviour. It should also be mentioned that the tangency condition in equation (6.2) implies that maximizing national income is the same as maximizing an aggregate utility function.

Corresponding to the utility function we now introduce two concepts: first, that of the indirect utility function, and second the expenditure function. These have been discussed earlier in these lecture notes. We first define the indirect utility function. Assume that the consumer has maximized utility subject to a budget constraint and that his/her demand functions are denoted by $X_i^*(i=1,2)$. These demand functions depend on prices and income, hence, the indirect utility function can be written as:

$$V = V(P_1, P_2, I) = V\left(X_1^*(P_1, P_2, I), X_2^*(P_1, P_2, I)\right) \tag{6.3}$$

where I denotes nominal income. The indirect utility function V is non-increasing in prices, P_1, P_2 and non-decreasing in income, I. In certain problems it is more elegant and useful to use V rather than U. The indirect utility function can be used to perform all the functions that are accomplished by using the direct form, for example, the function can be used to generate the ordinary demand curves by using Roy's Identity.

In addition to the indirect utility function the concept of an expenditure function is also widely used. This function is derived by minimizing expenditure subject to a specified level of utility at a given level of prices. It is denoted as:

$$e = e\left[P_1, P_2; \overline{U}\right] \tag{6.4}$$

where e denotes expenditure at prices given by P_1 and P_2 such that the specified level of utility $\overline{U}$ is attained. The expenditure function is concave, linearly homogenous and, by Shephard's lemma, its partial derivatives provide the Hicksian or income compensated demand functions.

In a closed economy supply must equal demand. Therefore we require that:

$$X_1 = Y_1 \tag{6.5}$$
$$X_2 = Y_2 \tag{6.6}$$

where $Y_i(i=1,2)$ and $X_i(i=1,2)$ denote the output and demand for commodities 1 and 2 respectively.

It is appropriate now to specify the production side of the economy. The production relationship for the *i*th good is written as:

$$Y_i = F_i(K_i, L_i),\ i = 1,2 \tag{6.7}$$

where K_i and L_i denote the amount of capital and labour allocation to the *i*th industry. Note that we have assumed the absence of externalities in specifying equation (6.7). It is assumed that the production function satisfies the conditions of homogeneity of degree one, indispensability of factors of production and the Inada conditions. Given homogeneity, the production function in its intensive form is given below:

$$Y_i = L_i F_i\left(\frac{K_i}{L_i}, 1\right) = L_i f_i(k_i), \quad i = 1,2 \tag{6.8}$$

The Inada conditions are:

$$\lim_{k_i \to 0} f'(k_i) = \infty$$
$$\lim_{k_i \to \infty} f'(k_i) = 0$$

where $f'(k_i)$ denotes the marginal product of capital in the *i*th sector. The intensive form of the production function is widely used in trade and growth literature and will be utilized in several chapters.

Both the factor and commodity markets are assumed to be perfectly competitive. Given the further assumption of profit maximization and an interior solution, it follows in equilibrium that the reward of each factor equals the value of its marginal product. These are now defined in real terms. Good Y_1 has been taken as the numeraire. Hence,

$$r = f'(k_1) = Pf_2'(k_2) \tag{6.9}$$
$$w = f_1(k_1) - k_1 f_1'(k_1) = P[f_2(k_2) - k_2 f_2'(k_2)] \tag{6.10}$$

where r denotes the rental on capital, w the wage rate and $P = P_2/P_1$ the relative price ratio. Later in the book the bracketed (k_i) will be dropped from the functions for notational convenience. From equations (6.9) and (6.10) it follows that the ratio of factor rewards, ω, equals:

$$\omega(k_i) = \frac{w}{r} = \frac{f_i(k_i)}{f_i'(k_i)} - k_i,$$

$$i = 1,2 \text{ where } \omega = \frac{w}{r} \text{ (wage – rental ratio)} \tag{6.11}$$

These equilibrium conditions can also be written in an alternative form by exploiting the homogeneity property. By using this property the unit isoquants are expressed as:

$$1 = F_i\left[\frac{K_i}{Y_i}, \frac{L_i}{Y_i}\right] = F_i[a_{Ki}, a_{Li}] \quad i = 1,2 \tag{6.12}$$

where the $a_{ij}s$ denote the Leontief variable input coefficients. The two-sector model in the a_{ij} notation can be written in terms of the following equations:

$$c^1[w,r] = a_{L1}(w,r)w + a_{K1}(w,r)r = 1 \tag{6.13}$$
$$c^2[w,r] = a_{L2}(w,r)w + a_{K2}(w,r)r = P \tag{6.14}$$

In the equations below, the dependence of $a_{ij}s$ on the factor prices has been dropped for mathematical convenience.

The terms c^1 and c^2 depict the cost functions which are concave in w and r. Equations (6.13) and (6.14) clearly show that the $a_{ij}s$ are functions of the wage and rental rates. Given factor price flexibility, it follows that the two inelastically supplied factors of production are fully employed:

$$L_1 + L_2 = a_{L1}Y_1 + a_{L2}Y_2 = \overline{L} \tag{6.15}$$
$$k_1L_1 + k_2L_2 = a_{K1}Y_1 + a_{K2}Y_2 = \overline{K} \tag{6.16}$$

This model assumed that the aggregate supplies of labour and capital are given exogenously and that these inputs can be allocated between the sectors in a costless manner. In more general models the factor supplies can be made endogenous.

To complete the presentation of the dual side of the model one more concept needs to be introduced. It is the notion of a revenue function. In a two sector model there are two commodities Y_1 and Y_2, and two inelastically supplied factors of production, capital K and labour L. The revenue function is the maximized value of $P_1Y_1 + P_2Y_2$ subject to the constraints of technology and factor endowments. Thus:

$$\underset{Y_1, Y_2}{\text{Max}} P_1Y_1 + P_2Y_2 = P_1F_1(K_1, L_1) + P_2F_2(K_2, L_2)$$

subject to:

$$L_1 + L_2 = \overline{L}$$
$$K_1 + K_2 = \overline{K}$$

The formal solution to this problem provides us with optimal values of $K_i's$ and $L_i's$ in terms of factor prices and endowments and we can obtain the revenue function in terms of goods prices and factor endowments. Let this be denoted as:

$$R = R[P_1, P_2; \overline{K}, \overline{L}] \tag{6.17}$$

This function is convex in prices and concave in factor endowments. The function is also linear homogeneous in terms of the set of parameters ((P_1, P_2) and $(\overline{K}, \overline{L})$ taken separately). The revenue function has important and useful properties. These are given below:

(P1) $$\frac{\partial R}{\partial P_1} = R_1 = Y_1(P_1, P_2; \overline{K}, \overline{L}) = \text{supply function for } Y_1 \tag{6.18}$$

$$\frac{\partial R}{\partial P_2} = R_2 = Y_2(P_1, P_2; \overline{K}, \overline{L}) = \text{supply function for } Y_2 \tag{6.19}$$

(P2) $$\frac{\partial R}{\partial \overline{K}} = R_{\overline{K}} = r = \text{rental rate on capital} \tag{6.20}$$

$$\frac{\partial R}{\partial \overline{L}} = R_{\overline{L}} = w = \text{wage rate} \tag{6.21}$$

Thus, by differentiating the revenue function with respect to its arguments, $P_1, P_2, \overline{K}$ and $\overline{L}$ we can obtain the supply functions for Y_1, Y_2 and the rewards of factors of production r and w. By taking second order derivatives of the above functions we obtain:

(P3) $$\frac{\partial^2 R}{\partial P_1^2} = R_{11} = \frac{\partial Y_1(P_1, P_2; \overline{K}, \overline{L})}{\partial P_1} \geq 0 \tag{6.22}$$

$$\frac{\partial^2 R}{\partial P_2^2} = R_{22} = \frac{\partial Y_2(P_1, P_2; \overline{K}, \overline{L})}{\partial P_2} \geq 0 \tag{6.23}$$

(P4) $$\frac{\partial^2 R}{\partial \overline{K}^2} = R_{\overline{K}\overline{K}} = \frac{\partial r}{\partial \overline{K}} \leq 0 \qquad (6.24)$$

$$\frac{\partial^2 R}{\partial \overline{L}^2} = R_{\overline{L}\overline{L}} = \frac{\partial w}{\partial \overline{L}} \leq 0 \qquad (6.25)$$

Properties P3 and P4 follow from the assumption of the convexity of the revenue function in prices and concavity in endowments. The economic meaning of these conditions is that the supplies of output are non-decreasing in commodity prices and factor returns are non-increasing in factor supply. Note that we have now used most of the concepts from consumption and production theory in the two sector model of general equilibrium.

From Young's theorem (also known as the Samuelson reciprocity condition) it follows that:

(P5) $$\frac{\partial^2 R}{\partial P_1 \partial \overline{L}} = \frac{\partial^2 R}{\partial \overline{L} \partial P_1} \qquad (6.26)$$

Hence,

$$\frac{\partial w}{\partial P_1} = \frac{\partial Y_1}{\partial \overline{L}} \qquad (6.27)$$

$$\frac{\partial w}{\partial P_2} = \frac{\partial Y_2}{\partial \overline{L}} \qquad (6.28)$$

$$\frac{\partial r}{\partial P_1} = \frac{\partial Y_1}{\partial \overline{K}} \qquad (6.29)$$

and

$$\frac{\partial r}{\partial P_2} = \frac{\partial Y_2}{\partial \overline{K}} \qquad (6.30)$$

These relationships show the dual relations in the trade model and are nothing other than the Rybczynski-Stolper-Samuelson theorems. These will be discussed in detail in the Important Relationships section. This completes the specification of the two-sector general equilibrium model and its tools. We now proceed to provide a treatment of the important relationships in the two sector model. Note that now important duality is in economics as it can be used in many instances.

IMPORTANT RELATIONSHIPS

Given the restrictions on the production functions, it is obvious from Equation (6.11) that the capital-labour ratios, k_i (i=1,2) are uniquely determined by the wage-rental ratio. The relation between k_i and ω is obtained by differentiating Equation (6.11) with respect to ω:

$$\frac{\partial k_i}{\partial \omega} = -\frac{(f_i')^2}{f_i f_i''} > 0 \qquad i=1,2 \tag{6.31}$$

Equation (6.31) states that an increase in the wage-rental ratio results in an increase in the capital-labour ratio. The economic explanation follows from profit maximization (cost minimization) and the assumptions regarding the production functions. An increase in the wage-rental ratio represents an increase in the relative price of labour, so that profit maximizing firms substitute capital for labour, the relatively cheaper factor for the relatively dearer factor, leading to an increase in the capital-labour ratio.

Having established the monotonic and unique relation between the wage-rental ratio and the factor intensities, we now proceed to explore the relation between the relative price of commodities and the wage-rental ratio. From Equation (6.9) it follows that:

$$P = \frac{f_1'(k_1)}{f_2'(k_2)} \tag{6.32}$$

The right-hand side of Equation (6.32) is only a function of the wage-rental ratio ω. Let this function be denoted by $P(\omega)$. By differentiating $P(\omega)$ with respect to ω, we obtain:

$$\frac{\omega}{P}\frac{\partial P}{\partial \omega} = \frac{\omega(k_1 - k_2)}{(\omega + k_1)(\omega + k_2)} \tag{6.33}$$

From Equation (6.33) it is clear that $(\omega/P)(\partial P/\partial \omega)$ is positive or negative, according to whether k_1 is greater or less than k_2. Therefore, the wage-rental ratio and commodity price ratios are related to each other via the physical factor intensity of the two sectors.

We are now in a position to construct the back-to-back diagram in which the relation between factor intensity, wage-rental ratio and commodity prices are all presented in one diagram. In Figure 6.1 we present the above relationship. An explanation of Figure 6.1(a) and a heuristic explanation of the result contained in Equation (6.11) follows. In quadrant I, the interrelationship between capital intensities, k_1 and k_2, and the wage-rental ratio ω is represented. An increase in the wage-rental ratio results in an increase in the capital intensity in both sectors. This is shown by the curves k_1 and k_2. In quadrant II we present the relationship between the commodity – price ratio P and the wage-rental ratio ω. Given that $k_1 > k_2$, we know from Equation (6.33) that this is positive. The curve *AA* illustrates this relationship. The increase in the wage-rental ratio affects the relative price of the labour-intensive sector 2 proportionately more than that of the capital-intensive sector 1. Therefore, the relative price of commodity 2 rises more than that of commodity 1, hence, *AA* is positively sloped.

(a) Factor intensity, wage-rental ratio and commodity prices for $k_1 > k_2$

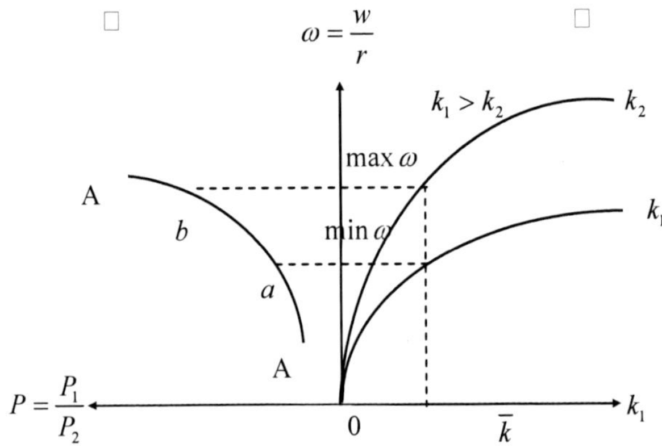

(b) Factor intensity, wage-rental ratio and commodity prices for $k_2 > k_1$

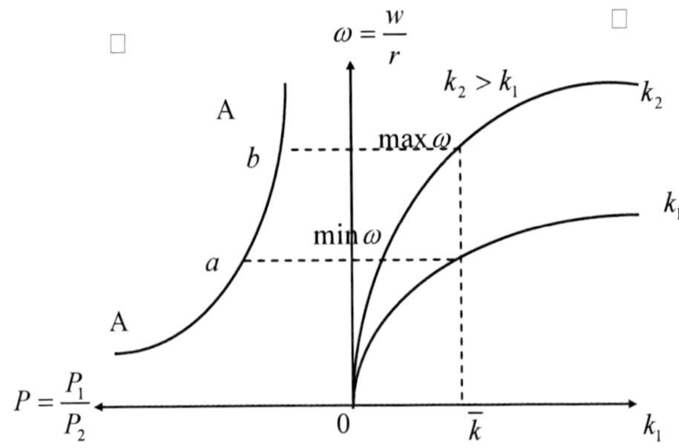

Figure 6.1

It is important here to draw attention to the fact that some points in Figure 6.1(a) are not feasible. The feasible points are obtained by imposing the full-employment condition on the model. Suppose the overall capital-labour ratio is given by $\bar{k}$. Let $O\bar{k}$ represent this ratio in Figure 6.1(a). It follows immediately that the range of variation (for incomplete specialization) in the wage-rental ratio is then given by points between minimum ω (min ω) and maximum ω (max ω). Obviously the economy is completely specialized in producing Y_1 if min ω prevails and in producing Y_2 if max ω becomes the established wage-rental ratio. The range of commodity price ratio for which the economy remains incompletely specialized is indicated by points that belong to the open internal $]a,b[$ that is, at points that are between *a* and *b* in quadrant II of Figure 6.1(a).

This section can be skipped and has been added for completeness

In this two sector general equilibrium model the most difficult relationship to derive is between the relative price ratio and the movements in the outputs as it involves most of the equations that have been presented. It is important to note here that this is not the case when duality is used. This relationship can be presented either by using primal (as in Hazari (1986)) or by using the dual and hat calculus. We will derive it from the latter. By differentiating Equations (6.15) and (6.16) we know that:

$$\lambda_{L1}\hat{Y}_1 + \lambda_{L2}\hat{Y}_2 = -[\lambda_{L1}\hat{a}_{L1} + \lambda_{L2}\hat{a}_{L2}] \tag{6.34}$$

$$\lambda_{K1}\hat{Y}_1 + \lambda_{K2}\hat{Y}_2 = -[\lambda_{K1}\hat{a}_{K1} + \lambda_{K2}\hat{a}_{K2}] \tag{6.35}$$

where ^ denotes proportional change and $\lambda_{ij}s$ the factor shares. By totally differentiating the relation that each $\lambda_{ij}s$ is a function of the wage rate and rental on capital, we obtain:

$$\hat{a}_{Li} = \frac{wc^i_{ww}(w,r)}{c^i_w(w,r)}\hat{w} + \frac{rc^i_{wr}(w,r)}{c^i_r(w,r)}\hat{r} \tag{6.36}$$

$$\hat{a}_{Ki} = \frac{rc^i_{rr}(w,r)}{c^i_r(w,r)}\hat{r} + \frac{wc^i_{rw}(w,r)}{c^i_w(w,r)}\hat{w} \tag{6.37}$$

We know from microeconomics theory that the cost functions, c^i, are linearly homogeneous; hence, it follows that their derivatives, c^i_w, c^i_r are homogenous of degree zero. Hence,

$$wc^i_{ww} + rc^i_{wr} = 0 \tag{6.38}$$

$$rc^i_{rr} + wc^i_{rw} = 0 \tag{6.39}$$

We now define the elasticity of substitution in alternative but equivalent ways:

$$\sigma = \frac{\hat{K} - \hat{L}}{\hat{w} - \hat{r}} = \frac{(\hat{K} - \hat{Y}) - (\hat{L} - \hat{Y})}{\hat{w} - \hat{r}} = \frac{\hat{a}_K - \hat{a}_L}{\hat{w} - \hat{r}}$$

$$= \frac{c^i(\cdot)c^i_{rw}(\cdot)}{c_w(\cdot)c_r(\cdot)} \tag{6.40}$$

By using the above equation it can be easily established that:

$$\hat{a}_{Li} = -\theta_{Ki}\sigma_i(\hat{w} - \hat{r}) \tag{6.41}$$

$$\hat{a}_{Ki} = -\theta_{Li}\sigma_i(\hat{w} - \hat{r}) \tag{6.42}$$

where $\theta_{Ki} = ra_{Ki}/P_i$ and $\theta_{Li} = wa_{Li}/P_i$, that is the relative shares of capital and labour in the price of good i.

By differentiation Equations (6.13) and (6.14) and the use of hat calculus we obtain:

$$\theta_{L1}\hat{w} + \theta_{K1}\hat{r} = 0 \tag{6.43}$$

$$\theta_{L2}\hat{w} + \theta_{K2}\hat{r} = \hat{P} \tag{6.44}$$

by solving Equations (6.43) and (6.44) we obtain:

$$\hat{w} = -\frac{\theta_{K1}\hat{P}}{|\theta|} \tag{6.45}$$

and

$$\hat{r} = \frac{\theta_{L1}\hat{P}}{|\theta|} \tag{6.46}$$

where $|\theta| = \theta_{L1}\theta_{L2}(k_2 - k_1)$. Hence, $|\theta| > 0(< 0)$ as $k_2 - k_1 > 0(< 0)$.

From Equations (6.45) and (6.46) it is clear that:

$$\hat{w} - \hat{r} = -\frac{\hat{P}}{|\theta|} \tag{6.47}$$

We are now in a position to re-write Equations (6.34) and (6.35) in the following manner:

$$\lambda_{L1}\hat{Y}_1 + \lambda_{L2}\hat{Y}_2 = \beta_L\hat{P} \tag{6.48}$$

$$\lambda_{K1}\hat{Y}_1 + \lambda_{K2}\hat{Y}_2 = -\beta_K\hat{P} \tag{6.49}$$

where

$$\beta_L = \lambda_{L1}\theta_{K1}\sigma_1 + \lambda_{L2}\theta_{K2}\sigma_2 > 0$$

and

$$\beta_K = \lambda_{K1}\theta_{L1}\sigma_1 + \lambda_{K2}\theta_{L2}\sigma_2 > 0.$$

By solving the system of equations (6.48) and (6.49) we obtain:

$$\hat{Y}_1 = -\frac{\lambda_{K2}\beta_L + \lambda_{L2}\beta_K}{|\theta||\lambda|}\hat{P} \tag{6.50}$$

$$\hat{Y}_2 = \frac{\lambda_{K1}\beta_L + \lambda_{L1}\beta_K}{|\theta||\lambda|}\hat{P} \tag{6.51}$$

where $|\lambda| = \lambda_{L1}\lambda_{L2}(k_2 - k_1) > 0$ and $|\theta| = \theta_{L1}\theta_{L2}(k_2 - k_1) > 0$.

From Equations (6.50) and (6.51) it is clear that $\hat{Y}_1 < 0$ and $\hat{Y}_2 > 0$, hence, the respective supply curves are upward sloping. Note that duality makes it very easy to establish that the supply curve is upward sloping.

DUALITY RELATIONS IN THE TWO-SECTOR MODEL

In this section we present two important propositions, the Rybczynski and the Stolper-Samuelson theorems, which are duals of each other. Consider the subsystem consisting of Equations (6.7)-(6.10) and (6.15)-(6.16). This subsystem consists of eight equations in eight unknowns: $Y_1, Y_2, L_1, L_2, k_1, k_2, w$ and r. We take P as given. This sub-system describes the production side of the economy. Two different questions can be posed about this system. First, what happens to outputs when factor endowments change (either $\overline{K}, \overline{L}$, or both) at constant commodity prices (constant P_1 and P_2 and in some interpretations P). These are known as factor endowment theorems. Second, what happens to factor prices when commodity prices change (either P_1, P_2 or both) and factor endowments are held constant (i.e. $\overline{K}$ and $\overline{L}$ are kept at a fixed level)? These are known as price-factor income relationships (theorems).

We shall first examine the factor endowment – output relationships and then take up the price-factor income relationship. Let us first consider the implication of an increase in the capital stock $\overline{K}$ on levels of output at constant prices. This can be accomplished by differentiating the production function with respect to $\overline{K}$. With prices held constant, it follows that the optimal capital-labour ratio will remain undisturbed as long as both industries have positive outputs. Hence, by differentiating Equations (6.7) with respect to $\overline{K}$, we obtain:

$$\frac{\partial Y_i}{\partial \overline{K}} = f_i \frac{\partial L_i}{\partial \overline{K}}, \quad i = 1,2 \tag{6.52}$$

and from the factor endowment conditions (6.15) and (6.16) we obtain:

$$\frac{\partial L_1}{\partial \overline{K}} = \frac{1}{(k_2 - k_1)} \tag{6.53}$$

$$\frac{\partial L_2}{\partial \overline{K}} = -\frac{1}{(k_2 - k_1)} \tag{6.54}$$

Substituting from Equations (6.53) and (6.54) into Equation (6.52) we obtain:

$$\frac{\partial Y_1}{\partial \overline{K}} = -\frac{f_1}{(k_2 - k_1)}, \quad \text{or} \quad \hat{Y}_1 = -\frac{\lambda_{K2}}{|\lambda|}\hat{K} \tag{6.55}$$

$$\frac{\partial Y_2}{\partial \overline{K}} = \frac{f_2}{(k_2 - k_1)}, \quad \text{or} \quad \hat{Y}_2 = \frac{\lambda_{L2}}{|\lambda|}\hat{K} \tag{6.56}$$

Similarly

$$\frac{\partial Y_1}{\partial \overline{L}} = \frac{k_2 f_1}{(k_2 - k_1)}, \quad \text{or} \quad \hat{Y}_1 = \frac{\lambda_{K2}}{|\lambda|}\hat{L} \tag{6.57}$$

$$\frac{\partial Y_2}{\partial \overline{L}} = -\frac{k_1 f_2}{(k_2 - k_1)}, \quad \text{or} \quad \hat{Y}_2 = -\frac{\lambda_{L2}}{|\lambda|}\hat{L} \tag{6.58}$$

From Equations (6.55)-(6.58), the Rybczynski theorem is easily obtained. Note that the alternative expressions in hat calculus have been derived by using the structure of the model written in terms of the unit cost equations.

Theorem 6.1 (Rybczynski theorem). *In an incompletely specialized two-factor, two-commodity economy, an increase in the endowment of any factor, at constant prices, results in an increase in the output of the industry that uses the factor intensively and a decrease in the output of the other industry.*

This is a remarkable theorem, for it shows that an increase in the endowment of a factor does not lead to an increase in all outputs, but to the contrary leads to an absolute increase (decline) in the output of one industry and a decline in the output of the other industry. The intuitive explanation of the above result can easily be brought out by analysing the following equation regarding the factor endowments (from Equations 6.16):

$$k_1\frac{L_1}{\overline{L}} + k_2\frac{L_2}{\overline{L}} = \frac{\overline{K}}{\overline{L}} = k, \quad \text{or} \quad k_1 l_1 + k_2 l_2 = k \tag{6.59}$$

Note that $l_1 + l_2 = 1$ where l_i (i =1,2) indicates the proportion of labour allocated to each sector, and therefore, are less than unity at the point of an interior equilibrium. If we suppose that $\hat{K}$ increases, then the expression on the right-hand side of the above equation (k) rises, hence, the left-hand side must also rise. At constant prices k_1 and k_2 cannot change, and hence, all adjustments must occur through changes in l_1 and l_2. Assuming that $k_1 > k_2$, then the only way the left-hand side can rise is through an increase in l_1 which implies that l_2 must fall. It is obvious from the production function for Y_2 that a decrease in l_2 with constant k_2 implies that the output of Y_2, the labour-intensive sector, must decline.

We now proceed to examine the relation between changes in individual (nominal) commodity prices and factor rewards. We have already established that an increase in the commodity price ratio results in an increase (decrease) in the wage-rental ratio if sector 1 is capital-intensive (labour-intensive) compared with sector 2 and that the elasticity of this relation is greater than -1 and less than 1.

Sometimes this is used as a version of the Stolper-Samuelson theorem. Another version of the Stolper-Samuelson theorem relates movements in individual (nominal) commodity prices to individual factor rewards rather than to the ratio of factor rewards. By differentiating Equations (6.9) and (6.10) logarithmically with respect to P_1 and P_2 we obtain:

$$\frac{\partial \log r}{\partial \log P_1} = -\frac{(k_1+\omega)}{(k_2-k_1)}, \quad \text{or} \quad \hat{r} = -\frac{\theta_{L2}\hat{P}_1}{|\theta|} \tag{6.60}$$

$$\frac{\partial \log r}{\partial \log P_2} = -\frac{(k_2+\omega)}{(k_2-k_1)}, \quad \text{or} \quad \hat{r} = -\frac{\theta_{L1}\hat{P}_2}{|\theta|} \tag{6.61}$$

$$\frac{\partial \log w}{\partial \log P_1} = -\frac{k_2(k_1+\omega)}{w(k_1-k_2)}, \quad \text{or} \quad \hat{w} = \frac{\theta_{K2}}{|\theta|}\hat{P}_1 \tag{6.62}$$

$$\frac{\partial \log w}{\partial \log P_2} = -\frac{k_1(k_2+\omega)}{w(k_1-k_2)}, \quad \text{or} \quad \hat{w} = -\frac{\theta_{K1}}{|\theta|}\hat{P}_2 \tag{6.63}$$

Equations (6.60)-(6.63) clearly demonstrate that the movements in individual factor rewards and individual commodity prices depend on the factor intensities of the two sectors. The hat calculus version of the theorems is derived from the unit cost equations. For example, an increase in the price of commodity 1 raises the rental on capital and lowers the wage rate provided $k_1 > k_2$. The reverse holds when $k_1 < k_2$. Moreover, the elasticity of these responses, specifically $\partial \log r / \partial \log P_1$ and $\partial \log w / \partial \log P_1$ are greater than 1 when $k_1 > k_2$ while $\partial \log r / \partial \log P_2$ and $\partial \log w / \partial \log P_2$ are less than 1 for $k_1 > k_2$. Similar results can be stated for $k_1 < k_2$.

We state the Stolper-Samuelson theorem below:

Theorem 6.2 (Stolper-Samuelson theorem). *In an incompletely specialized two-factor, two-commodity economy an increase in the price of any commodity raises the real reward of the factor used intensively in the production of the commodity of which the price has increased and decreases the reward of the other factor.*

This theorem is demonstrated diagrammatically in Figure 6.2 by the use of price isoquants. Let $P_1 = 1$ be the unit-price isoquant for commodity 1 and P_2 be the price isoquant for commodity 2. These isoquants show the combinations of wage and rental on capital such that the same price is maintained along the entire isoquant. The point of intersection between the two isoquants provides the initial equilibrium values of r and w which are denoted by r^* and w^*. It is assumed that commodity Y_1 is capital intensive. Let us suppose that the price of the labour intensive good increases. This is shown by the shift in the price isoquant from P_2 to P_2'. At the new equilibrium point as shown by e' the rental on capital falls from r to r^{**} and the wage rises from w to w^{**}. Furthermore, the marginal product of labour rises in terms of both the commodities and the marginal product of capital falls in terms of both commodities. This is indeed a remarkable result because of the way in which it avoids the index number problem in obtaining the impact of a change in commodity price on factor rewards. However, it is difficult to avoid the index number problems in more generalized models where there are many factors and goods.

Having established both the Rybczynski and the Stolper-Samuelson results our remaining task is to show that the theorems are duals of each other.

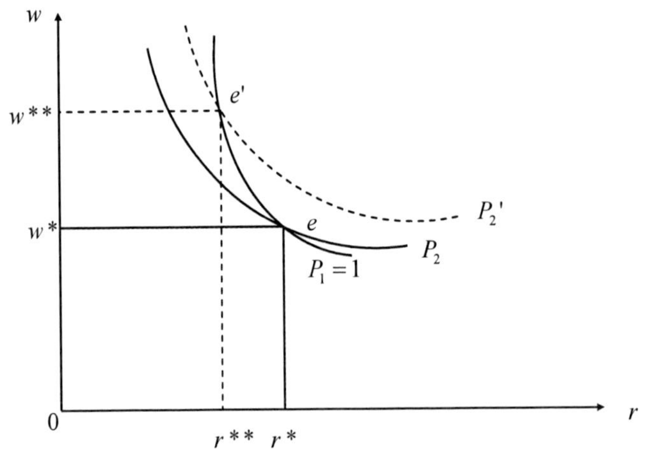

Figure 6.2. Factor prices

$$\frac{\partial w}{\partial P_j} = \frac{\partial Y_j}{\partial \bar{L}}, \qquad j = 1,2 \tag{6.64}$$

and

$$\frac{\partial r}{\partial P_j} = \frac{\partial Y_j}{\partial \bar{K}}, \qquad j = 1,2 \tag{6.65}$$

This is a very neat demonstration of duality relationship. We presented duality in consumption and production before and now we have shown it in general equilibrium.

THE PRODUCTION POSSIBILITY CURVE

We have presented above the major results of a two-sector model of an economy. However, all this has been achieved without introducing the production possibility curve (also known as the transformation curve). Many results in various areas of economic use are either proved or illustrated with the help of the production possibility surface. In this section we take a digression to establish this concept. The production possibility curve shows the various combinations of the two commodities, which might be produced under certain market conditions. Given our assumption of competitive markets, it represents the maximum possible output of one commodity given the output of the other that is $Y_1 = Y_1(Y_2)$.

This section may be skipped

The production possibility curve is generally derived with the help of the Edgeworth-Bowley box diagram.[3] Since the two factors of production are fixed in supply, a box can be constructed, as in Figure 6.3, the dimensions of which represent the total supply of factors of production. Given our assumptions about the nature of production functions, the level of output can be measured by the distances of their isoquants from the respective origin. The diagonal $0_1 0_2$ measures the overall capital-labour ratio, $k = \overline{K}/\overline{L}$. This diagram plays an important role in the derivation of the production possibility schedule. Each point of a particular isoquant represents the same level of output, and hence, the output of each commodity can be measured by the intersection between the isoquant and the diagonal of the box. For example, the output of the first commodity Y_1, represented by isoquant Y_1 and Y_1', is indicated by $0_1 a_1$ and $0_1 a_1'$, respectively. The points $0_2 b_2$ and $0_2 b_2'$ can be interpreted in a similar manner. Given these interpretations of points along the diagonal, a movement away from 0_1 towards 0_2, represents an increase in the output of the first commodity Y_1 and a decline in the output of the second commodity Y_2 and vice versa.

By introducing the Pareto optimality criterion, the contract locus and the production possibility curve is derived. This criterion states that a production point is efficient if every other feasible reallocation of inputs results in a decrease in the output of at least one commodity. In view of this criterion, efficiency in the allocation of the two resources labour and capital can be attained at points such as *A* and *C*, where the isoquants of the two-commodities are tangential to each other. The locus of all tangency points, the curve $0_1 AC0_2$, is called the contract curve or the efficiency locus.

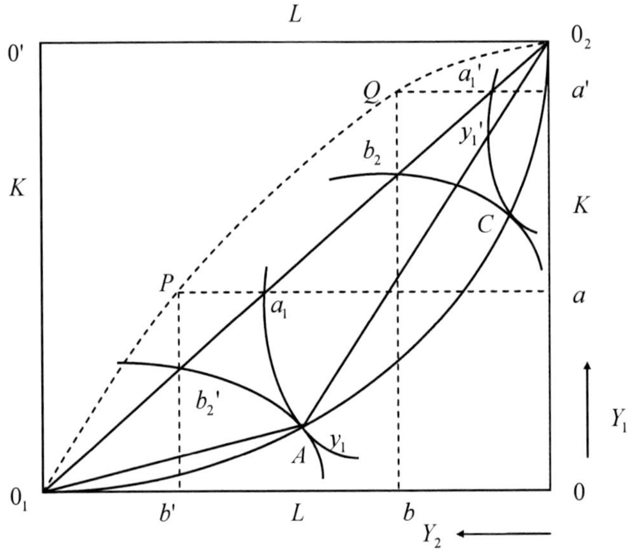

Figure 6.3. From the Edgeworth-Bowley box diagram to the production possibility frontier

The position of the contract curve in the box depends on the assumption regarding the capital intensity of the two sectors. The contract curve in the diagram lies below the diagonal because of our assumption that sector Y_2 is capital-intensive relative to sector Y_1. Hence, the slope of 0_1A (the capital-labour ratio in Y_1) with respect to the 0_10 axis is less than the capital-labour ratio in Y_2, which is given by the slope of 0_2A with respect to $0_20'$ axis. If, instead of Y_2, Y_1 was the capital-intensive commodity, then the contract curve would be entirely above the diagonal. If the capital intensities of the two sectors are identical, then the diagonal in effect becomes the contract curve and also the production possibility locus.

The production possibilities curve can be derived from the contract curve. We have already established that various points on the diagonal represent different levels of output of each commodity. If we transform this measuring scale to the vertical and the horizontal axis with the origin *0*, the transformation curve can be obtained. For example, the output levels of Y_1, given by points a_1 and a_1' on the diagonal, can be projected towards the 00_2 axis to points a_1 and a', respectively. Since the production functions are assumed to be homogeneous of degree one, the distance $0_1a_1'$ is in exactly the same proportion by which $0a'$ exceeds $0a$. Similarly the output of Y_2 can be projected to obtain the points on the horizontal and vertical axis. The output associated with point *A* is given, respectively, by $0a$ and $0b'$. The output combination given by points *a* and b' determines the point *P* in the commodity space. In similar fashion the output combination at *C* is associated with point *Q* in the output space. The locus of all such points is called the production possibility curve, which is given by 0_1PQ0_2. The production possibility curve is concave towards the origin. This is due to our assumption of constant returns to scale, differences in the factor intensity of the two sectors and the applications of Pareto optimality criterion. Note that if $k_1 = k_2$ then the economy has a straight-line transformation curve as stated earlier.

So far we have concentrated on deriving the shape of the production possibility locus.

Read from here if you have skipped the marked section

We now determined the point at which production equilibrium occurs. By differentiating Equation (6.7) totally, we obtain:

$$dY_1 = \frac{\partial F_1}{\partial K_1} dK_1 + \frac{\partial F_1}{\partial L_1} dL_1$$

and

$$dY_2 = \frac{\partial F_2}{\partial K_2} dK_2 + \frac{\partial F_2}{\partial L_2} dL_2$$

From Equations (6.9) and (6.10), we know that $r = (\partial F_1/\partial K_1) = P(\partial F_2/\partial K_2)$ and that $w = (\partial F_1/\partial L_1) = P(\partial F_2/\partial L_2)$. It also follows from the full employment conditions that $dL_2 = -dL_1$ and $dK_2 = -dK_1$. By making appropriate substitutions, we obtain:

$$-\frac{dY_1}{dY_2} = DRT = P$$

where $-dY_1/dY_2$ represents the slope of the production possibility schedule and is defined as the domestic rate of transformation (DRT).

The condition derived above shows that in competitive equilibrium the slope of the production possibility curve equals the commodity-price ratio. This also equals the slope of the social indifference curve as at a point of utility maximization the ratio of marginal utilities, DRS, also equals *P*, hence, DRS=DRT=*P*.

On the basis of Figure 6.4 it is very easy to establish the existence of a competitive equilibrium. Consider Figure 6.5. We show the equilibrium position in terms of three graphs. In Figure 6.5 panel I the production possibility curve *TT* is drawn. Every point on the production possibility curve is a point of profit maximization. We are using social indifference curves to depict consumer preferences. The system reaches a point of equilibrium at point *e* where the slope of the social indifference curve (DRS) equals the slope of the production possibility curve (DRT) which in turn equals the closed economy equilibrium price ratio (*P*) given by the slope of the line *AB*. Now this is a competitive equilibrium as:

(i) Firms maximize profits subject to the constraints of the technology.

(ii) Consumers maximize utility subject to the budget constraint.

and

(iii) Excess demand equals zero.

(a) Autarky equilibrium

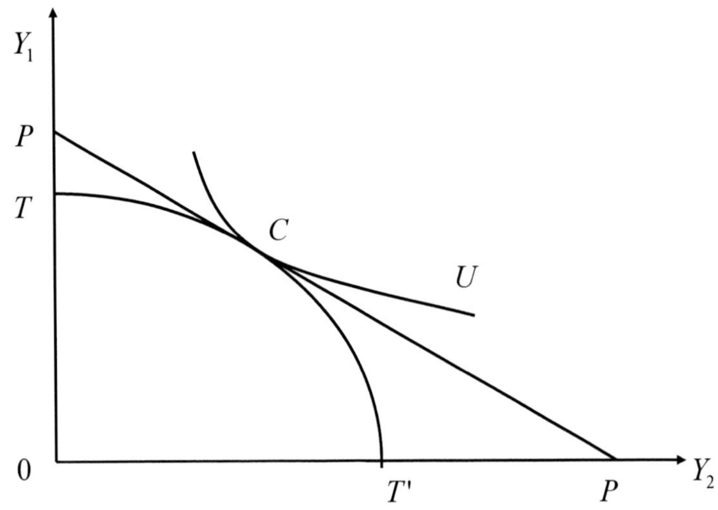

(b) Free trade equilibrium

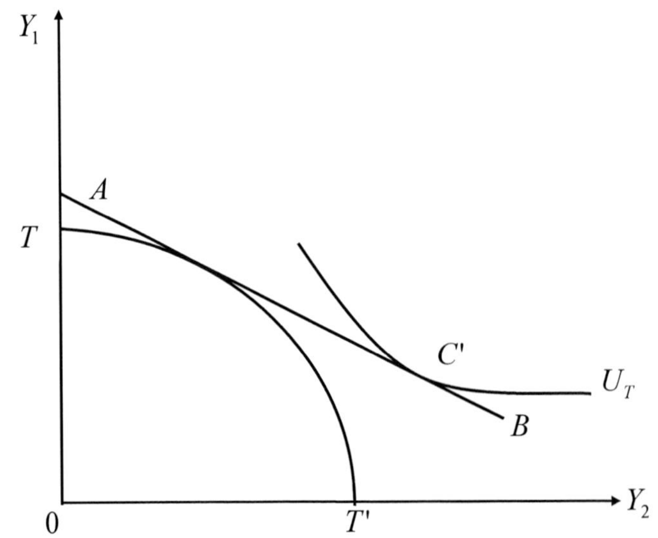

Figure 6.4

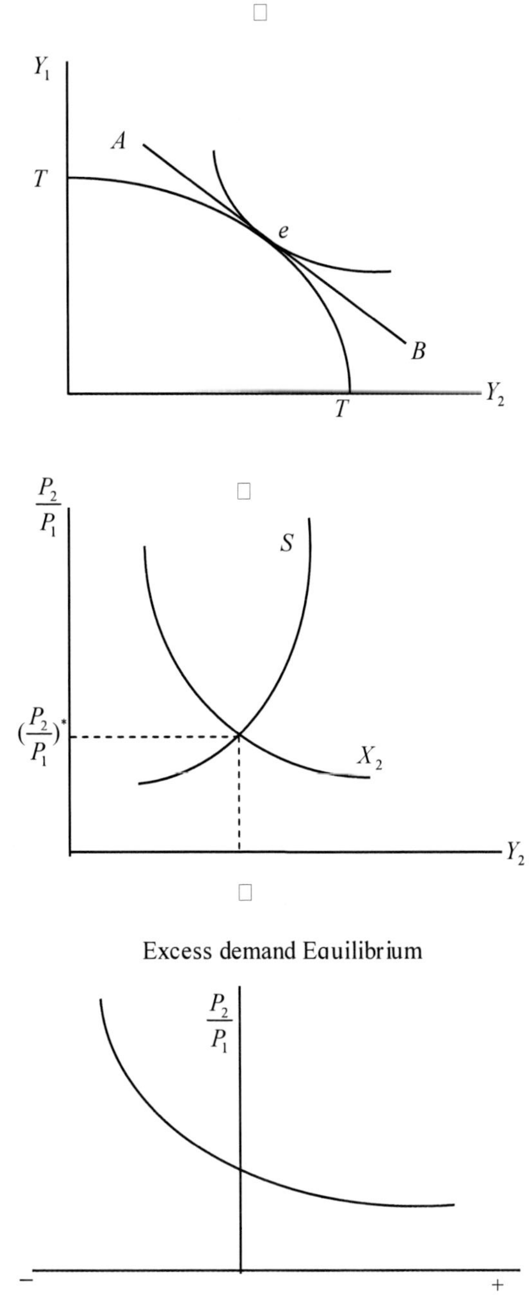

Figure 6.5

Note that it is also Pareto optimal. In the background the marginal rates of substitution for all consumers are equal to the commodity price ratio given by the slope of price line *AB*.

How does Brover fixed point theorem work for this case? The existence theorem would start from Figure 6.5 panel III. In this panel we have drawn the continuous excess demand function for commodity 2, that is:

$$Z_2(P) = X_2 - Y_2$$

Since both Y_2 and X_2 are continuous Z_2 is also continuous. The prices can be normalized and after that like the notes on exchange the function *g* can be constructed to apply the Brower fixed point theorem. Note that we have to clear only one market. This method of teaching general equilibrium is constructive as it shows how general equilibrium models work. One can increase the generality of these models by introducing *n* goods, *n* factors and endogenized supply of factors. But the proofs rely heavily on arriving at continuous excess demand functions, normalization so that the simplex can be used and then applying the fixed point theorem.

Notes

1. See the paper by Samuelson (1956) on this issue.
2. Duality is easily defined in terms of sets and propositions relating to these sets. Consider sets *A* and *B* and operators α and β on these sets. If a given proposition is valid, then sometimes it might be possible to obtain a second valid proposition from it by interchanging the sets (*B* for *A*) and the two operators (β for α) as well. Mathematically this states that $\alpha A \leftrightarrow \beta B$. This is satisfied in the case of Rybczynski and Stolper-Samuelson theorems. When this is possible, we usually refer to the original propositions as the primal and the second as its dual. The Rybczynski and Stolper-Samuelson theorems satisfy the duality relationship.
3. This technique was first introduced by Savosnick (1958).

Chapter 7

EXTERNALITIES*

(written by Bharat Hazari and Shuang Yao)

Jean Jacques Laffont (1989) produced a beautiful but difficult treatment of externalities in his book on public sector economics. It is marvelous in terms of technique used and is general enough to cover most topics related to the theory of externalities. French economists (many of them trained as engineers and mathematicians) have a habit of producing results in a complex way. Laffont's treatment is in this French tradition and in this Chapter we will make it as easy as possible to understand it by using the tools borrowed from trade theory. Trade theory provides a general treatment of distortions. This general framework is capable of handling many types of externalities and this Chapter uses this framework to present several results.

A MODEL WITH EXTERNALITIES

We consider an economy that produces two goods Y_1 and Y_2 with the help of inelastically supplied mobile labour and sector specific capital. The presence of an externality is defined to be present when the well being of a consumer or the production function of a firm (industry) are affected directly by the actions of other agents in the economy. The term directly is used to clearly show that the price mechanism is not involved in the interaction among various agents. We assume that the output of sector 2, Y_2, is affected by the presence of externalities: The externalities are generated from the consumption of good 1 (X_1) and from the production of good 1 (Y_1). The production functions for these goods are given below:

$$Y_1 = F_1(L_1, \overline{K_1}) \tag{7.1}$$

* This chapter is dedicated to the memory of my friend, Jean Jacques Laffont.

$$Y_2 = F_2(L_2, \overline{K_2}, Y_1, X_1) \tag{7.2}$$

The production functions are assumed to be strictly concave in $L_i (i = 1, 2)$. The specific factors $K_i (i = 1, 2)$ are fully used in the respective sectors. Sector 2 suffers from externalities as represented by the presence of Y_1 and X_1 in the production function for commodity 2. These can be either positive or negative. We shall assume that the system is characterized by a negative externality, that is, $\partial Y_2 / \partial Y_1 < 0$ and $\partial Y_2 / \partial X_1 < 0$. In Figure 7.1 we demonstrate how the externality has an effect on the total product curve of labour in sector 2. The functions are assumed to be twice differentiable. An example of such an externality could be pollution generated by production of Y_1 as well as consumption of this good. The representative consumer has a utility function which is assumed to be twice differentiable and strictly concave, that is:

$$U = U(X_1, X_2) \tag{7.3}$$

Where U denotes utility and $X_i (i = 1,2)$ the consumption of the two goods.

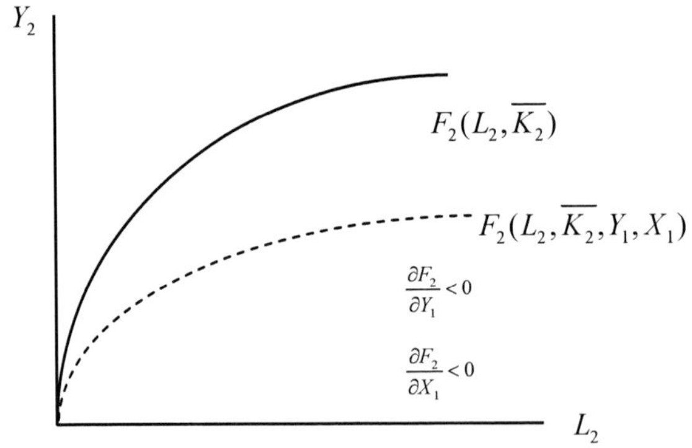

Figure 7.1

As all factor prices are assumed to be flexible the system is in full employment equilibrium so that $L_1 + L_2 = \overline{L}$. It should be pointed out that in Laffont's treatment there are no primary factors of production.

Further it is assumed that commodity 1 is imported and commodity 2 is exported, hence, market clearing requires that:

$$X_1 = Y_1 + M_1 \tag{7.4}$$

$$X_2 = Y_2 - E_2 \tag{7.5}$$

where M_1 and E_2 denotes the imports and exports of good 1 and 2 respectively.

The country is assumed to be small, hence, the terms of trade $P = (P_2 / P_1)$ are given exogenously. The balance-of-payments condition requires that:

$$PE_2 = M_1 \tag{7.6}$$

Equation (7.6) states that the value of exports equals the value of imports. Note that we have set up an open economy model. The advantage of such a model is that by making the small country assumption price movements can be ignored.

This completes the specification of the model for the purpose of this chapter.

THE DERIVATION OF THE OPTIMALITY CONDITIONS IN THE PRESENCE OF AN EXTERNALITY

We follow the procedure of Laffont and first derive the Pareto Optimum given the presence of the externality. The Pareto Optimum conditions for this system can be obtained by solving the following problem:

$$Max U(X_1, X_2)$$

Subject to:

$$Y_1 = F_1(L_1, \overline{K_1})$$

$$Y_2 = F_2(L_2, \overline{K_2}, Y_1, X_1)$$

$$L_1 + L_2 = \overline{L}$$

$$X_1 = Y_1 + M_1$$

$$X_2 = Y_2 - E_2$$

$$PE_2 = M_1$$

The Lagrangian of this system is given below on the assumption that the system has an interior solution:

$$G = U(X_1, X_2) + \lambda_1[-Y_1 + F_1(L_1, \overline{K_1})] + \lambda_2[-Y_2 + F_2(L_2, \overline{K_2}, Y_1, X_1)]$$
$$+ \lambda_3(-L_1 - L_2 + \overline{L}) + \lambda_4(-X_1 + Y_1 + M_1)$$
$$+ \lambda_5(-X_2 + Y_2 - E_2) + \lambda_6(PE_2 - M_1) \tag{7.7}$$

By differentiating G with respect to $X_1, X_2, L_1, L_2, Y_1, Y_2, M_1$ and E_2 we obtain:

$$\frac{\partial G}{\partial X_1} = \frac{\partial U}{\partial X_1} + \lambda_2 \frac{\partial F_2}{\partial X_1} - \lambda_4 = 0 \tag{7.8}$$

$$\frac{\partial G}{\partial X_2} = \frac{\partial U}{\partial X_2} - \lambda_5 = 0 \tag{7.9}$$

$$\frac{\partial G}{\partial L_1} = \lambda_1 \frac{\partial F_1}{\partial L_1} - \lambda_3 = 0 \tag{7.10}$$

$$\frac{\partial G}{\partial L_2} = \lambda_2 \frac{\partial F_2}{\partial L_2} - \lambda_3 = 0 \tag{7.11}$$

$$\frac{\partial G}{\partial Y_1} = -\lambda_1 + \lambda_2 \frac{\partial F_2}{\partial Y_1} + \lambda_4 = 0 \tag{7.12}$$

$$\frac{\partial G}{\partial Y_2} = -\lambda_2 + \lambda_5 = 0 \tag{7.13}$$

$$\frac{\partial G}{\partial M_1} = \lambda_4 - \lambda_6 = 0 \tag{7.14}$$

$$\frac{\partial G}{\partial E_2} = -\lambda_5 + \lambda_6 P = 0 \tag{7.15}$$

By eliminating the Lagrange multipliers we obtain the condition for Pareto Optimality:

$$\frac{\dfrac{\partial U}{\partial X_2}}{\dfrac{\partial U}{\partial X_1} + \dfrac{\partial U}{\partial X_2}\dfrac{\partial F_2}{\partial X_1}} = P = FRT = \frac{\dfrac{\partial F_1}{\partial L_1}}{\dfrac{\partial F_2}{\partial L_2} - \dfrac{\partial F_2}{\partial Y_1}\dfrac{\partial F_1}{\partial L_1}} \tag{7.16}$$

This equation shows that at the point of a Pareto Optimum the true domestic rate of substitution equals the foreign rate of transformation, which in turn equals the true domestic rate of transformation.

Let us first examine the term for the social marginal rate of substitution. The numerator of this term gives the marginal utility derived from the consumption of good 2. The denominator of the expression consists of two terms: $\partial U/\partial X_1$ (marginal utility from consumption of good 1) and the externality term $((\partial U/\partial X_2)(\partial F_2/\partial X_1))$. This consists of the standard marginal utility term $(\partial U/\partial X_2)$ which is multiplied by the effect of the consumption of good 1 on production of good 2. The rate of social substitution must take account of this effect.

Next let us examine the term for the social marginal rate of transformation from the production side. By increasing one unit of labour employment in sector 1 and decreasing one unit of labour employment in sector 2 we obtain additional $\partial F_1/\partial L_1$ unit of good 1 which is shown in the numerator, and this additional production of good 1 consequently affect the production of good 2 by $(-(\partial F_2/\partial Y_1)(\partial F_1/\partial L_1))$. Thus, this operation totally decreases the production of good 2 by $(\partial F_2/\partial L_2 - (\partial F_2/\partial Y_1)(\partial F_1/\partial L_1))$ unit which is shown in the denominator. It consists of two terms: the marginal product of labour in sector 2, $\partial F_2/\partial L_2$ and the externality term $(-(\partial F_2/\partial Y_1)(\partial F_1/\partial L_1))$.

In a model with international trade the domestic rate of substitution (DRS) must equal the foreign rate of transformation (FRT) which in turn equals the domestic rate of transformation (DRT). In trade theory the following distortions are defined:

(1) $DRS = DRT \neq FRT$ Foreign distortion

(2) $DRS = FRT \neq DRT$ Domestic distortion

(3) $DRS \neq DRT = FRT$ Domestic distortion

and

(4) Shrinkage of the production possibility locus.

These distortions can be shown to prevail in a very wide variety of models. We will show that these can be used in the literature on externalities.

Equation (7.16) shows that the true DRS equals the foreign rate of transformation and that in turn equals the true domestic rate of transformation. The first best solution (absence of externalities) follows from Equation (7.16) by setting $(\partial F_2/\partial X_1)=0$ and $(\partial F_2/\partial Y_1)=0$ which gives us:

$$\frac{\frac{\partial U}{\partial X_2}}{\frac{\partial U}{\partial X_1}}=P=\frac{\frac{\partial F_1}{\partial L_1}}{\frac{\partial F_2}{\partial L_2}}=-\frac{dY_1}{dY_2} \tag{7.17}$$

or

$$DRS=FRT=DRT$$

Competitive Equilibrium

In this section we consider an equilibrium derived from the behavior of individual agents maximizing their objective functions subject to constraints. We commence our analysis by considering the consumer first. The representative consumer maximizes utility subject to a budget constraint, hence:

$$\underset{X_1,X_2}{Max}\,U(X_1,X_2)$$

Subject to

$$P_1X_1+P_2X_2=I$$

where I denotes total income of the representative consumer. From the first order conditions we obtain:

$$\frac{\dfrac{\partial U}{\partial X_2}}{\dfrac{\partial U}{\partial X_1}} = \frac{P_2}{P_1} = P \qquad (7.18)$$

which states that the ratio of marginal utilities equals the price ratio.

Let us now consider sector 1. In this sector the profit maximization problem consists of the following:

$$\underset{L_1}{Max}\, P_1F_1(L_1,\overline{K}_1) - WL_1 - r\overline{K}_1$$

The maximization of the above yields:

$$\frac{\partial F_1}{\partial L_1} = \frac{W}{P_1} \qquad (7.19)$$

Note how this links with Chapter 3 of these lecture notes.

Finally, we consider the maximization problem in sector 2 given the level of externalities $\overline{Y}_1$ and $\overline{X}_1$:

$$\underset{L_2}{Max}\, P_2F_2\left(L_2,\overline{K}_2,\overline{Y}_1,\overline{X}_1\right) - WL_2 - r\overline{K}_2$$

This maximization yields:

$$\frac{\partial F_2}{\partial L_2} = \frac{W}{P_2} \qquad (7.20)$$

From Equations (7.19) and (7.20) we obtain:

$$\frac{\partial F_1 / \partial L_1}{\partial F_2 / \partial L_2} = \frac{P_2}{P_1} \qquad (7.21)$$

A competitive equilibrium with externalities is a vector of an allocation $\left(\overline{Y}_1, \overline{Y}_2, \overline{X}_1, \overline{X}_2, \overline{L}_1, \overline{L}_2, \overline{M}_1, \overline{E}_2, W, r\right)$ at the terms of trade *P*. This allocation satisfies the following:

(a) In sector 2 profits are maximized given $P, r, W, \overline{Y}_1$ and $\overline{X}_1$.
(b) In sector 1 profits are maximized given *P*, *r* and *W*.
(c) The representative consumer maximizes utility subject to a budget constraint.
(d) All markets clear at the internationally given price ratio *P*.

It is clear that a competitive equilibrium in our context is not Pareto Optimal as the individual agents equate their private marginal rates of substitution or transformation rather than social rates to the price ratio as shown below:

$$\frac{\dfrac{\partial U}{\partial X_2}}{\dfrac{\partial U}{\partial X_1} + \dfrac{\partial U}{\partial X_2}\dfrac{\partial F_2}{\partial X_1}} = P = \frac{\dfrac{\partial F_1}{\partial L_1}}{\dfrac{\partial F_2}{\partial L_2} - \dfrac{\partial F_2}{\partial Y_1}\dfrac{\partial F_1}{\partial L_1}} \neq \frac{\dfrac{\partial U}{\partial X_2}}{\dfrac{\partial U}{\partial X_1}} = P = \frac{\dfrac{\partial F_1}{\partial L_1}}{\dfrac{\partial F_2}{\partial L_2}} \qquad (7.22)$$

The social rates are shown on the left hand side of the inequality and private rates on the right hand side.

Before obtaining an optimal solution by use of property rights, taxes and so on we illustrate our results with geometry.

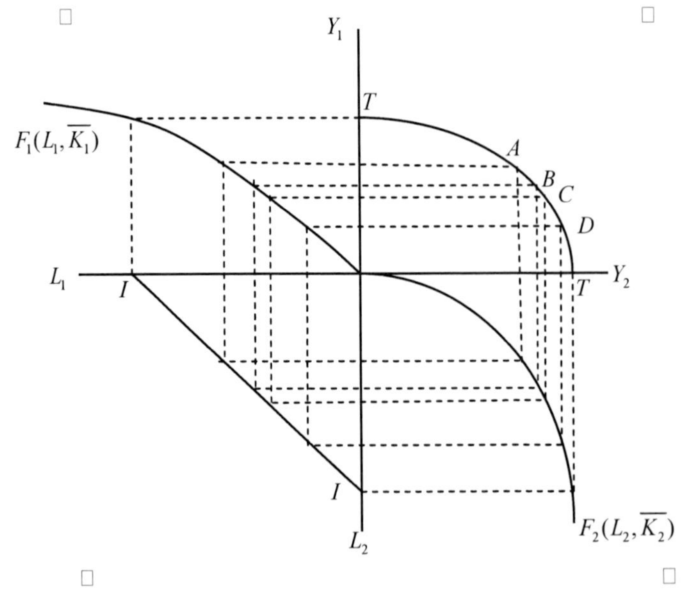

Figure 7.2

In Figure 7.2 we demonstrate the production possibility curve without presence of externalities TABCDT. In quadrant I the labour constraint is drawn and in quadrant II and IV the total product curves of labour in sectors 1 and 2 respectively. In sector 2 the total product curve $F_2(L_2, \overline{K}_2)$ represents the situation without externality.

In Figure 7.3 negative externalities push the total product curve of labour in sector 2 inwards to $F_2(L_2, \overline{K_2}, Y_1^i, X_1^i)$ $(i = a, b, c, d)$ with $Y_1^a > Y_1^b > Y_1^c > Y_1^d$ and $X_1^a > X_1^b > X_1^c > X_1^d$. Externalities cause the production possibility curve to shrink from TABCDT to TabcdT. It would be easy to construct an example where the production possibility set could become non-convex a point made by Starrct in a seminal paper on the relation between externalities and convexity of sets. Figure 7.3 shows how this non-convexity happens geometrically. However, for our purpose we shall retain the assumption that the production set remains strictly convex.

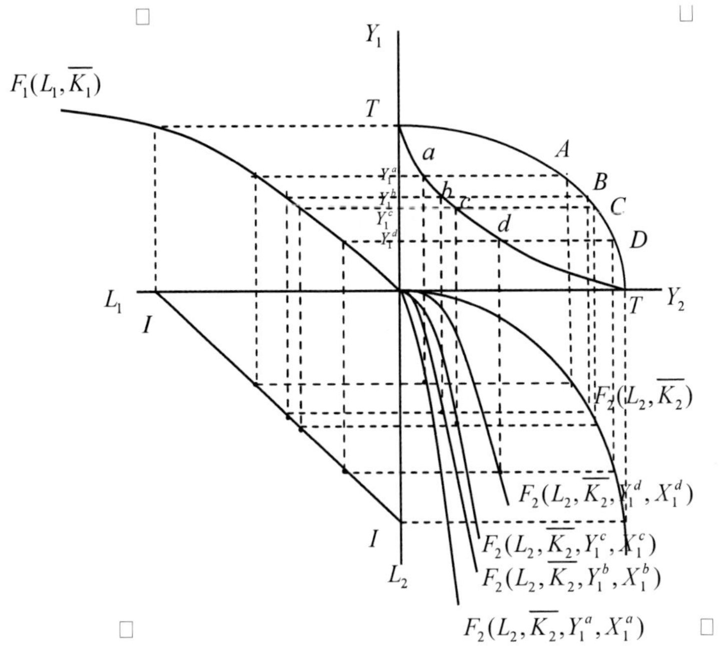

Figure 7.3

In Figure 7.4, the first best solution (competitive equilibrium with optimality) is obtained at the point where the commodity price ratio is tangent to the PPC (a locus with no externality) and the social indifference curve U and on this the standard trade theory result holds that *DRS=DRT=FRT*. Production occurs at *P* and consumption at *C*.

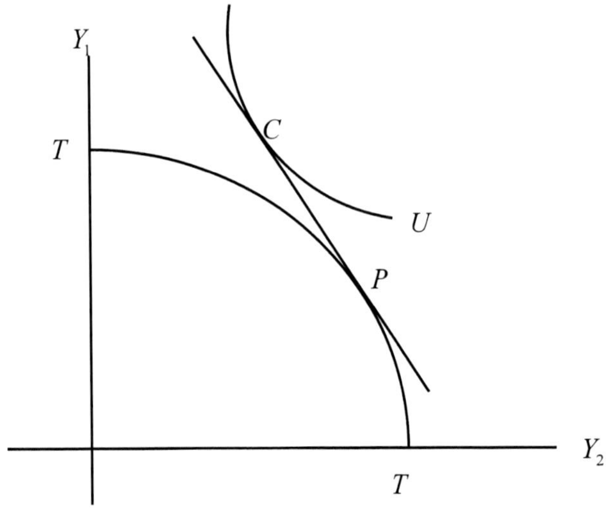

Figure 7.4

In Figure 7.5, the competitive equilibrium with the externality occurs on the shrunken PPC. Welfare level is shown by the indifference curve $U' < U$. Production occurs at point P' and consumption at C'. We notice that since $(-(\partial F_2 / \partial Y_1)(\partial F_1 / \partial L_1)) > 0$, at the point P' where agents equate their private rates to the price ratio.

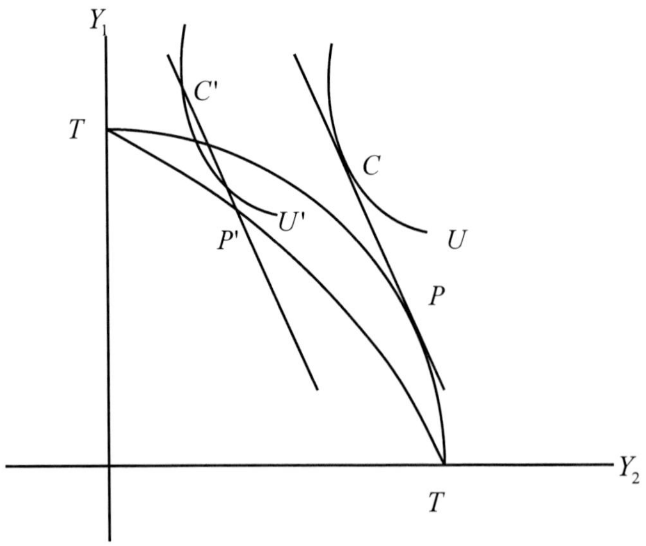

Figure 7.5

$$\text{True}\quad DRT = \frac{\dfrac{\partial F_1}{\partial L_1}}{\dfrac{\partial F_2}{\partial L_2} - \dfrac{\partial F_2}{\partial Y_1}\dfrac{\partial F_1}{\partial L_1}} < \frac{\dfrac{\partial F_1}{\partial L_1}}{\dfrac{\partial F_2}{\partial L_2}} = P = FRT$$

At the point C' since $((\partial U/\partial X_2)(\partial F_2/\partial X_1)) < 0$,

$$True\; DRS = \frac{\dfrac{\partial U}{\partial X_2}}{\dfrac{\partial U}{\partial X_1} + \dfrac{\partial U}{\partial X_2}\dfrac{\partial F_2}{\partial X_1}} > \frac{\dfrac{\partial U}{\partial X_2}}{\dfrac{\partial U}{\partial X_1}} = P = FRT$$

Optimal Policies

In the previous section we have established that a competitive equilibrium is not Pareto optimal in the presence of an externality. In this section we consider various types of intervention. The first type of intervention we consider is creating property rights. The establishment of such rights creates markets and there by the externality is internalized. Property rights are embedded in sector 2. Hence, sector 1 must buy from sector 2 the right to pollute. Let this price be denoted by q_1. Firms in sector 1 now undertake the following maximization exercise:

$$\underset{L_1}{Max}\, P_1F_1(L_1,\overline{K}_1) - WL_1 - q_1F_1(L_1,\overline{K}_1)$$

The first order condition for the above maximization is

$$P_1\frac{\partial F_1}{\partial L_1} - W - q_1\frac{\partial F_1}{\partial L_1} = 0$$

or

$$\frac{\partial F_1}{\partial L_1} = \frac{W}{P_1 - q_1} \tag{7.23}$$

Equation (7.23) shows that the effective wage has increased as $(P_1 - q_1) < P_1$. This increase in the effective wage rate reduces the amount of labour hired, hence, the output of Y_1 falls from where it would have been at price P_1

In a similar manner the consumer must buy the right to pollute from sector 2. Let the price for this right to pollute be denoted by q_1^c. The consumers' maximization problem now becomes:

$$Max U(X_1, X_2)$$

subject to

$$P_1 X_1 + P_2 X_2 + q_1^c X_1 = I$$

Maximization leads to the following solution:

$$\frac{\partial U / \partial X_2}{\partial U / \partial X_1} = \frac{P_2}{P_1 + q_1^c} \tag{7.24}$$

The right hand side of equation (7.24) shows that the effective price of commodity 1 has increased as $P_1 + q_1^c > P_1$, hence, consumer reduces the amount of X_1 he / she consumes.

We are now in a position to write the maximization problem for the firm in sector 2:

$$Max P_2 F_2(L_2, \overline{K_2}, Y_1, X_1) - W L_2 + q_1 Y_1 + q_1^c X_1$$

The first order conditions for the above maximization are:

$$P_2 \frac{\partial F_2}{\partial L_2} - W = 0 \tag{7.25}$$

$$P_2 \frac{\partial F_2}{\partial Y_1} + q_1 = 0 \tag{7.26}$$

$$P_2 \frac{\partial F_2}{\partial X_2} + q_1^c = 0 \tag{7.27}$$

We also require that the supply of pollution rights equals the demand for these rights — so that the market clears. Combining these equations yields the following result:

$$DRS = \frac{\dfrac{\partial U}{\partial X_2}}{\dfrac{\partial U}{\partial X_1} + \dfrac{\partial U}{\partial X_2}\dfrac{\partial F_2}{\partial X_1}} = \frac{1}{\dfrac{\partial U / \partial X_1}{\partial U / \partial X_2} + \dfrac{\partial F_2}{\partial X_1}}$$

$$= \frac{1}{\dfrac{P_1 + q_1^c}{P_2} - \dfrac{q_1^c}{P_2}}$$ [use equations (7.24) and (7.27)]

$$= \frac{P_2}{P_1} = FRT$$

$$DRT = \frac{\dfrac{\partial F_1}{\partial L_1}}{\dfrac{\partial F_2}{\partial L_2} - \dfrac{\partial F_2}{\partial Y_1}\dfrac{\partial F_1}{\partial L_1}} = \frac{\dfrac{W}{P_1 - q_1}}{\dfrac{W}{P_2} + \dfrac{q_1}{P_2}\dfrac{W}{P_1 - q_1}}$$ [use (7.23), (7.25) and (7.26)]

and $$= \frac{1}{\dfrac{P_1 - q_1}{P_2} + \dfrac{q_1}{P_2}}$$

$$= \frac{P_2}{P_1} = FRT$$

Thus

$$DRS = FRT = DRT$$

We demonstrate this result in Figure 7.6. The price ratio is tangent to the social indifference curve U'' on the shrunken PPC. Production occurs at point P'' and consumption at C''. We note that the consumption of commodity 1 at point C'' is lower than at C' and the production of Y_1 at point P'' is lower than at P'. Welfare level is shown by the indifference curve $U' < U'' < U$. Note that pollution has not gone to zero but to an optimal level. Political parties fail to understand that the optimal solution does not imply zero output of an industry and zero consumption by a consumer.

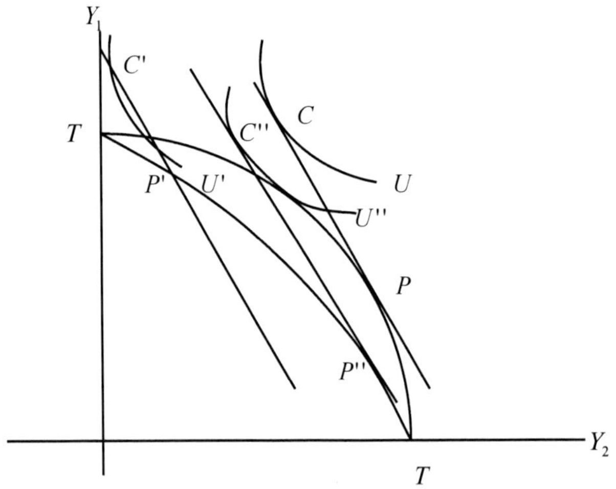

Figure 7.6

Optimal Taxation

Another way of arriving at the optimal solution is by using taxes. Let us normalize $P_1 = 1$. We assume that the consumer pays a tax t per unit of good 1 consumed and the firms in sector 1 pay a tax τ per unit of good 1 produced. This is a standard way of handling the externalities in this type of modeling. The tax revenue is distributed to the consumer in a lump-sum manner $\overline{T} = \tau Y_1 + tX_1$, and considered by the consumer to be independent of his own choices.

Now firms in sector 1 undertake the following maximization exercise:

$$\underset{L_1}{Max}\, F_1(L_1, \overline{K}_1) - WL_1 - \tau F_1(L_1, \overline{K}_1)$$

The first order condition is:

$$\frac{\partial F_1}{\partial L_1} = \frac{W}{1-\tau} \tag{7.28}$$

The consumers' maximization problem now becomes:

$$\underset{X_1,X_2}{Max}\, U(X_1, X_2)$$

Subject to

$$(1+t)X_1 + PX_2 = I + \overline{T}$$

This maximization yields:

$$\frac{\partial U / \partial X_2}{\partial U / \partial X_1} = \frac{P}{1+t} \tag{7.29}$$

The maximization problem for the firms in sector 2 is:

$$\underset{L_2}{Max}\; PF_2(L_2, \overline{K_2}, Y_1, X_1) - WL_2$$

This maximization yields:

$$\frac{\partial F_2}{\partial L_2} = \frac{W}{P} \tag{7.30}$$

By using the procedure already outlined we obtain:

$$\tau^* = -P\frac{\partial F_2}{\partial Y_1} \qquad t^* = -P\frac{\partial F_2}{\partial X_1}$$

Adding this to equations (7.28), (7.29) and (7.30) we construct the conditions parallel to equations (7.23)-(7.27) with P_1 being normalized.

Thus Pareto optimum can again be established on the shrunken locus.

Integration of Firms

Other solutions to externalities can be found such as integration of firms when consumption externality is absent, that is,

$$\frac{\partial F_2}{\partial X_1} = 0$$

The first order condition for the consumer is easy to obtain:

$$\frac{\partial U / \partial X_2}{\partial U / \partial X_1} = \frac{P_2}{P_1}$$

The integration of the both sectors results in the following joint profit maximization problem:

$$Max P_1 Y_1 - WL_1 + P_2 Y_2 - WL_2$$

Subject to

$$Y_1 = F_1(L_1, \overline{K_1})$$
$$Y_2 = F_2(L_2, \overline{K_2}, Y_1)$$

The maximization of the above problem yields:

$$P_1 \frac{\partial F_1}{\partial L_1} + P_2 \frac{\partial F_2}{\partial Y_1} \frac{\partial F_1}{\partial L_1} = W$$

$$P_2 \frac{\partial F_2}{\partial L_2} = W$$

The combination of the above two equations provides us:

$$\frac{\dfrac{\partial F_1}{\partial L_1}}{\dfrac{\partial F_2}{\partial L_2} - \dfrac{\partial F_2}{\partial Y_1}\dfrac{\partial F_1}{\partial L_1}} = \frac{P_1}{P_2}$$

Again we establish the Pareto optimal condition in equation (7.16) with $\dfrac{\partial F_2}{\partial X_1} = 0$.

POLLUTION ABATEMENT

Another solution to externality when consumption externality is absent is pollution abatement. Denote as z the amount of pollution. The pollution abatement techniques applied by the firms in sector 1 are modeled as follows:

$$z = \phi(Y_1, d) \text{ with } z = \phi(Y_1, 0)$$

where d denotes the cost of good 1 to decrease the pollution of Y_1 .

The Pareto optimum condition for this system can be obtained by solving the following problem:

$$Max\, U(X_1, X_2)$$

Subject to

$$\begin{aligned}
&Y_1 = F_1(L_1, \overline{K_1}) \\
&Y_2 = F_2(L_2, \overline{K_2}, \phi(Y_1, d)) \\
&L_1 + L_2 = \overline{L} \\
&X_1 = Y_1 + M_1 \\
&X_2 = Y_2 - E_2 \\
&PE_2 = M_1
\end{aligned}$$

The first order condition characterize the above optimal problem is:

$$\frac{\frac{\partial U}{\partial X_2}}{\frac{\partial U}{\partial X_1}} = P = \frac{1}{\frac{\partial F_2}{\partial z}\frac{\partial \phi}{\partial d}} = \frac{\frac{\partial F_1}{\partial L_1}}{\frac{\partial F_2}{\partial L_2} - \frac{\partial F_2}{\partial z}\frac{\partial \phi}{\partial Y_1}\frac{\partial F_1}{\partial L_1}}$$

Let the pollution be taxed at the rate τ and pollution abatement be subsidized at the rate γ.

The firms in sector 1 now face the following maximization problem:

$$Max P_1 Y_1 - WL_1 - \tau z + \gamma d$$

Subject to

$$Y_1 = F_1(L_1, \overline{K_1})$$
$$z = \phi(Y_1, d)$$

The above maximization yields:

$$\frac{\partial F_1}{\partial L_1} = \frac{W}{P_1 - \tau \frac{\partial \phi}{\partial Y_1}} \tag{7.31}$$

The maximization problem for the firms in sector 2 becomes:

$$Max P_2 Y_2 - WL_2$$

Subject to

$$Y_2 = F_2(L_2, \overline{K_2}, z)$$

The first order condition is:

$$\frac{\partial F_2}{\partial L_2} = \frac{W}{P_2} \tag{7.32}$$

We obtain the result:

$$\frac{\frac{\partial F_1}{\partial L_1}}{\frac{\partial F_2}{\partial L_2}-\frac{\partial F_2}{\partial z}\frac{\partial \phi}{\partial Y_1}\frac{\partial F_1}{\partial L_1}}=\frac{\frac{W}{P_1-\tau\frac{\partial \phi}{\partial Y_1}}}{\frac{W}{P_2}-\frac{\partial F_2}{\partial z}\frac{\partial \phi}{\partial Y_1}\frac{W}{P_1-\tau\frac{\partial \phi}{\partial Y_1}}} \quad \text{[use (7.31),(7.32)]}$$

$$=\frac{1}{\frac{P_1-\tau\frac{\partial \phi}{\partial Y_1}}{P_2}-\frac{\partial F_2}{\partial z}\frac{\partial \phi}{\partial Y_1}}$$

$$=\frac{1}{\frac{P_1+P_2\frac{\partial F_2}{\partial z}\frac{\partial \phi}{\partial Y_1}}{P_2}-\frac{\partial F_2}{\partial z}\frac{\partial \phi}{\partial Y_1}} \quad (\tau=-P_2\frac{\partial F_2}{\partial z})$$

$$=\frac{P_2}{P_1}$$

Consumers' maximization problem is:

$$Max\,U(X_1,X_2)$$

Subject to

$$P_1X_1+P_2X_2=I$$

The first order condition is:

$$\frac{\partial U/\partial X_2}{\partial U/\partial X_1}=\frac{P_2}{P_1}$$

Again, the Pareto optimum condition (7.16) is satisfied with the consumption externality being absent.

This treatment is a very simple way of analyzing the externalities problems posed by Laffont. All the results obtained can be demonstrated by geometry and analyzed in terms of standard trade and distortion theory.

Chapter 8

SIMULTANEOUS GAMES

In the previous chapters we discussed both consumers and producers make their decisions in competitive market in which consumers maximize utility and producers maximize profits at given market prices subject to economic constraints. How much utility or profit they receive is independent of decisions made by other economic agents in the market. However, if we relax the assumption of perfect competition, then an economic agent in general has to consider the actions of other agents in his own decision. This gives rise to multi-person decision making.

Strategic interaction involves at least two agents who make decisions that affect one another's payoff. This can be modeled as a game played by two or more agents. Game theory, after all, provides an analytical framework to help us logically solve the game to find any equilibrium outcome(s). There are mainly two types of games: **simultaneous games** and **sequential games**. In this chapter we will focus on simultaneous games in which there is complete information. In a simultaneous game, all players (economic agents) make decisions at the same time or in the situation they do not know the decisions of other players. Complete information in this context is defined as the players know the payoff functions of each other. In game theory literature, there is a study on simultaneous games are also analyzed with incomplete information but that is beyond the scope of this book.

PRISONERS' DILEMMA

Prisoners' Dilemma is a classic example to motivate the study of strategic interaction and to illustrate an application of game theory to find the solution(s) to a strategic problem. Suppose two suspects are arrested and charged with a crime and the police hold them in different cells. The police do not have sufficient evidence to convict either of them for charges unless one or both confess to the crime. We use the **strategic form** representation (Table 8.1) to describe the game. In principle, there are three elements by which a game is defined: a) The number of players, b) The strategies available to each player, and c) The payoffs to each player for every feasible combination of strategies.

Table 8.1 is a bi-matrix with two rows and two columns as in the game of Prisoners' Dilemma there are a) two players and b) each player has two strategies. In this game, the players are Prisoner A and Prisoner B. Each player has two strategies, {Confess} and {Not Confess}. A pair of strategies with the first strategy represents the strategy of the row player

(Prisoner A) and the second strategy represents the strategy of the column player (Prisoner B). The payoff to the row player is the first numeric value and the payoff to the column player is the second numeric value in a particular cell. For example, if a pair of strategy is (Confess, Not Confess) where Prisoner A chooses {Confess} and Prisoner B chooses {Not Confess}, then the payoff to Prisoner A is 0 and Prisoner B is -5.

Table 8.1 The game of Prisoners' Dilemma

		Prisoner B	
		Confess	Not Confess
Prisoner A	Confess	-3, -3	0, -5
	Not Confess	-5, 0	-1, -1

How to solve this dilemma or find the solution(s) of this game? Unlike the situation of perfect competition, in which an economic agent takes the market price as given without considering the decisions of other agents and solves his constrained maximization problem; in the situation of strategic interaction, what a strategy a player chooses depends on the strategies other players would choose. We illustrate this idea in the game of Prisoners' Dilemma. Since this is a game of complete information, so both players know the strategies available for each other and the payoffs of different pairs of strategies to each other. Prisoner A knows that Prisoner B can choose {Confess} or {Not Confess}, and vice versa. Suppose Prisoner B chooses {Confess} then Prisoner A will choose {Confess} since the payoff of choosing {Confess} is higher than {Not Confess} (-3 > -5); if Prisoner B chooses {Not Confess} then Prisoner A will also choose {Confess} since choosing {Confess} he gets 0 but -1 otherwise. Given this game is symmetric so Prisoner B will also have the same strategies. Therefore, no matter what the opponent would choose, it is always true that choosing {Confess} dominates {Not Confess}. In other words, {Confess} is a **dominant strategy** for both players and thus (Confess, Confess) is the solution to the game of Prisoners' Dilemma.

This solution appears counter-intuitive as both players are better off at the pair of strategies (Not confess, Not confess) rather than (Confess, Confess). Why don't the players choose {Not Confess} to obtain a higher payoff? Are the players irrational? No, both players are rational, and the rationality leads to this equilibrium outcome. Suppose if both players choose {Not Confess} to achieve a higher payoff from -3 to -1, then a rational player has an incentive to deviate from this pair of strategies to choose {Confess} to enjoy an increase in his own payoff from -1 to 0. Hence, driven by rationality to maximize an individual payoff, each player has an incentive to deviate from the pair of strategies, (Not Confess, Not Confess), to obtain an increase in his own payoff. Therefore, (Confess, Confess) is a pair of strategies such that no single player has an incentive to deviate from the equilibrium outcome.

This classic example illustrates how to formulate a strategic-form game and how to solve the game to find an equilibrium strategy. If the players are **rational,** they will choose the dominant strategy and the resulting outcome is a **dominant strategy equilibrium**. However, in most games there are no dominant strategies for both players, so what is the outcome in such games? To answer this problem we have to introduce the concept of Nash Equilibrium.

NASH EQUILIBRIUM

Nash Equilibrium is defined to be a pair of strategies such that the strategy of each player is a best response to the strategy of other players.

Table 8.2

		Ruby: Left	Ruby: Right
Ricky	Top	3, 1	0, 2
	Middle	2, 3	2, 1
	Bottom	2, 1	3, 2

Table 8.2 depicts a strategic-form game in which there are two players, Ricky and Ruby. The feasible strategies of Ricky are {Top, Middle, Bottom} and that of Ruby are {Left, Right}. We can easily establish that both Ricky and Ruby do not have a dominant strategy. However, we can find a Nash Equilibrium in this game. From the perspective of Ricky, if Ruby chooses {Left}, the best response for him is to choose {Top} and his payoff of this pair of strategies (Top, Left) is underlined; if Ruby chooses {Right}, the best response for him is to choose {Bottom} and his payoff of (Right, Bottom) is underlined. On the other hand, from the perspective of Ruby, if Ricky chooses {Top}, the best response for her is to choose {Left}; if Ricky chooses {Middle}, the best response for her is to choose {Left}; if Ricky chooses {Bottom}, the best response for her is to choose {Right}. Hence, (Bottom, Right) is a pair of strategies for which payoffs to both Ricky and Ruby are underlined. In other words, (Bottom, Right) is only one pair of strategies such that they are best response to each other, and therefore is a Nash Equilibrium.

The Nash Equilibrium, (Bottom Right) is stable because neither player has an incentive to unilaterally deviate from this pair of strategies. Suppose Ruby deviates her strategy from {Right} to {Left}, but this strategy is not the best response to {Bottom} if Ruby correctly anticipates that Ricky chooses {Bottom}. Also, if Ricky deviates from {Bottom} to {Middle}, this strategy is not the best response to {Right} if Ricky correctly anticipates Ruby chooses {Right}. Hence, if such anticipations are correct, (Bottom, Right) is only pair of strategies such that there is no single player deviates from his or her strategy unilaterally.

Table 8.3.

		Prisoner B: Confess	Prisoner B: Not Confess
Prisoner A	Confess	-3, -3	0, -5
	Not Confess	-5, 0	-1, -1

In the game of Prisoners' Dilemma as depicted in Table 8.3, (Confess, Confess) is Nash Equilibrium. A player's choice {Confess} is a best reply to both the choices of {confess} and {not confess} of another player. Hence, (Confess, Confess) is the unique pair of strategies such that the strategy of each player is a best response to the strategy of other players. Importantly, this example shows that a dominant strategy is always a Nash equilibrium strategy.

Multiple Nash Equilibria or No Nash Equilibrium

Both Ricky and Ruby prefer having dinner together to eating dinner separately. However, Ricky prefers Chinese food to Japanese food, whereas Ruby prefers Japanese food to Chinese food. The strategic-form game in Table 8.4 shows the preferences of Ricky and Ruby and the payoffs of every feasible pairs of actions. In this game we can find that there are two Nash Equilibria, (Chinese food, Chinese food) and (Japanese food, Japanese food). This example shows us that the solution of a game is not necessarily unique.

Table 8.4

		Ruby	
		Chinese food	Japanese food
Ricky	Chinese food	2, 1	0, 0
	Japanese food	0, 0	1, 2

Consider the case of a penalty kick match between two soccer teams. Suppose a kicker in team A has to shoot and a goalkeeper in team B has to defend the goal. The kicker can either shoot the ball to the left or the right of the goal; similarly, the goalkeeper can either jump to the left or the right of the goal. Hence, the feasible strategies of both kicker and goalkeeper are {Left} and {Right}. The game of penalty kick is a zero-sum game where the sum of payoffs to players is zero. If the kicker shoots the ball in the goal, then team A scores one point and team B loses one point. If the goalkeeper catches the ball, then both team A and team B neither gain nor lose a point. The details of the game are depicted in Table 8.5.

Table 8.5

		Goalkeeper	
		Left	Right
Kicker	Left	0, 0	1, -1
	Right	1, -1	0, 0

There is no Nash Equilibrium in this game. The kicker wishes to shoot the ball in the direction opposite to where the goalkeeper would jump; whereas the goalkeeper wants to jump in the direction where the kicker would shoot the ball. In other words, the objectives between the kicker and the goalkeeper are diametrically opposite; both players do not have a strategy that is a best response to each other's strategy in the sense that a single player has an incentive to unilaterally deviate from any pair of strategies.

Mixed Strategy

In the game of penalty kick, the kicker hopes that the goalkeeper can not anticipate the direction in which he will shoot the ball, and the goalkeeper hopes that the kicker can not anticipate the direction in which he will jump to the goal. This is because if the goalkeeper can correctly anticipate where the kicker would shoot the ball, then he will jump to the goal in that direction and save the goal. So, in reality, the kicker would randomly make a strategy so that the goalkeeper could not predict his strategy to take any advantages on him.

From the perspective of the kicker, if he always chooses {Left}, then the best response for the goalkeeper is to choose {Left} so that the goalkeeper can always save the gaol. In this situation, the kicker's strategy should be not to shoot to one side of the goal but to randomly shoot to any side to make it impossible for the goalkeeper to jump in the correct direction. In other words, the kicker should not play a **pure strategy** (a strategy chosen with certainty). To introduce randomness in shooting the ball, let p be the probability that the kicker chooses {Left}, then 1- p is the probability that the kicker chooses {Right}. The kicker should choose p such that the goalkeeper does not prefer to jump to one side. To find the optimal value of p, we have to make p such that the goalkeeper is indifferent between the payoff of choosing {Left} and {Right}. So,

$$(0)p+(-1)(1-p)=(-1)p+(0)(1-p)$$

$$p^* = 0.5$$

The left hand side of the above equation is the expected payoff of the goalkeeper to choose {Left} and the right hand side is the expected payoff of the goalkeeper to choose {Right}. Only when p^* = 0.5 the goalkeeper is indifferent between choosing {Left} and {Right}. In other words, rather than always shooting to one side, the kicker should shoot to the Left with a 50% chance and to the Right with a 50% chance so that the goalkeeper could not always catch the ball.

Similarly, let q be the probability that the goalkeeper chooses {Left} and 1- q the goalkeeper chooses {Right}, we find q^* = 0.5 to make the kicker indifferent between choosing {Left} and {Right}. Therefore, the kicker chooses {Left} with a 50% chance and the goal keeper chooses {Left} with a 50% chance is a pair of **mixed strategy** for which the strategy of each player is best response to the other's strategy.

COURNOT GAME

We close this chapter with an example to illustrate an application to the theory of the firm. Suppose there are two firms which produce a homogenous product with the output level of firm 1 denoted by y_1 and firm 2 by y_2, and $Y = y_1 + y_2$ is the output level in the industry.

The demand curve for the industry is given by $p = a - bY$, where p is the product's price. The cost functions of firm 1 and firm 2 are $c_1(y_1) = cy_1$ and $c_2(y_2) = cy_2$, where $c < a$.

Firm 1's profit maximization problem is $\max_{y_1} \pi_1(y_1, y_2) = [a - b(y_1 + y_2)]y_1 - cy_1$

and similarly

Firm 2's profit maximization problem is $\max_{y_2} \pi_2(y_1, y_2) = [a - b(y_1 + y_2)]y_2 - cy_2$

The above Cournot competition is a simultaneous game played by firm 1 and firm 2. Each firm simultaneously determines its own output (strategy) and its payoff (profit) depends on the level of output produced by another firm. Hence, solving the firm's profit maximization problem is to find the levels of output that are dependant upon the levels of output of another firm. The first-order condition for firm 1's profit maximization problem is:

$$\frac{\partial \pi_1(y_1, y_2)}{\partial y_1} = a - c - 2by_1 - by_2 = 0$$

The first-order condition for firm 1's determines that the profit-maximizing level of output of firm 1 is a function of all feasible levels of output that would be produced by firm 2. In other words, for each level of output produced by firm 1 is also a best response to the output that would be produced by firm 2. Such a relationship is called the **reaction function** of firm 1.

The first-order condition for firm 2's profit maximization problem is:

$$\frac{\partial \pi_1(y_1, y_2)}{\partial y_2} = a - c - 2by_2 - by_1 = 0$$

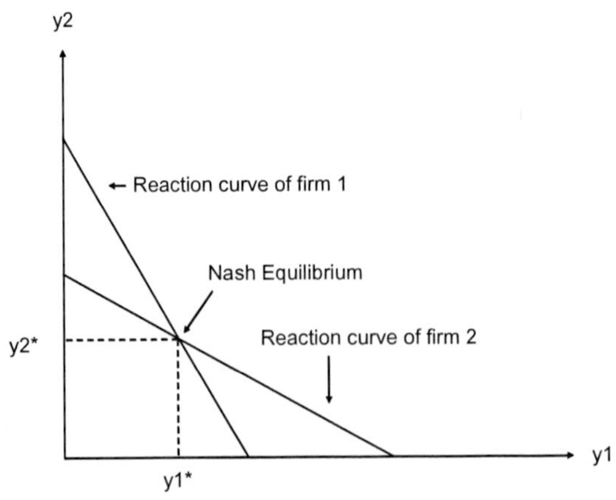

Figure 8.1

Nash Equilibrium is a pair of outputs such that the level of output of each firm is a best response to the output of each other. So by equating the reaction functions for firm 1 and firm 2, we find that the Nash Equilibrium level of output for firms 1 and firm 2 are $y_1^* = y_2^* = \frac{a-c}{3b}$ and depicted in Figure 8.1.

Chapter 9

SEQUENTIAL GAMES

In Chapter 8 we have analyzed simultaneous games in which players move simultaneously, or in the situation they do not know the decisions of each other. Therefore, the timing of decisions does not matter in such games. However, in reality, in some games two players make decisions sequentially in the sense that one player moves first and then another player moves afterwards, and that a player knows the previous decisions made by other players before making his own decision. Playing chess is an example. These are called **sequential games**. For this reason, the equilibrium outcomes of such games are different from that of simultaneous games. Therefore, we introduce **extensive-form** representation to describe sequential games and use **backward induction** analysis to refine the Nash Equilibrium concept.

We use the game of price war to motivate the study of sequential games. Suppose there is a monopolist in a computer industry and a new firm plans to enter the market. If the new firm does not enter the marker, then the incumbent firm can earn $10 profit and the new firm gets nothing. If the new firm enters the market, then the incumbent firm can start a price war against the new firm. If the incumbent firm starts a price war, then she gets $2 profit but the new firm loses $6. On the other hand, if the incumbent firm does not start a price war, both firms equally share the market and thus each firm gets $4 profit. To illustrate this sequential game we make use of **game tree**. The game is illustrated in Figure 9.1. Basically, a game tree is a diagram that describes the available choices of each player at each point in time. In a game tree, decision nodes represent the points at which players make a decision. In our game, the starting decision node is New Firm. Then, the branches connecting from a decision node represents the available choices of the player. Given that the new firm can either choose {Enter} or {Don't Enter}. Therefore, there are two branches connecting the decision node of the new firm. A branch either leads to another decision node or to a terminal node. Since the incumbent firm does not need to take any action if the new firm chooses {Don't Enter}, hence the game is finished in this case. The terminal node specifies the payoffs to both players. On the other hand, if the new firm chooses to enter the market, the incumbent firm has two choices, {Price War} and {No Price War}, at the decision node. The outcomes of the game are in the terminal nodes (end points) where the first value is the payoff to the new firm and the second value to the incumbent firm.

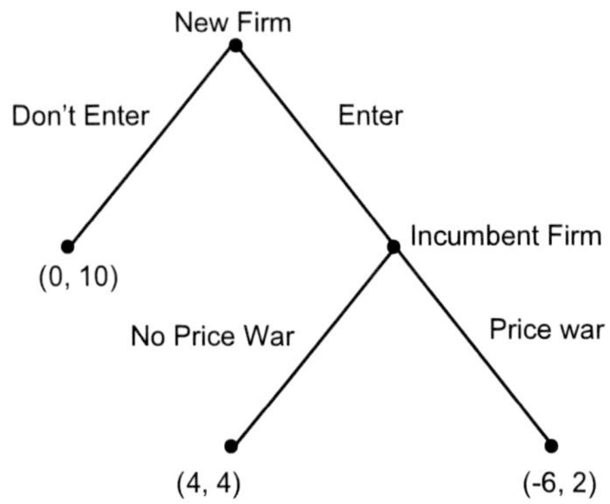

Figure 9.1 The Game of Price War

Formally, an extensive form representation of a game specifies 1) the players in the game, 2) what decision made by each player at what time, 3) what information received by each player, and 4) the payoffs to each player. The advantage of an extensive form representation is that it fully captures the dynamic structure of the game; we know when a player takes an action and what information received by a player for making his own decision.

To solve this game we have to specify the strategies available for each player. A strategy for a player specifies a complete list of actions and one action would be called upon to do under every decision node. So, what are the strategies available to the new firm in this game? Since there is one decision node for the new firm, the strategies for the new firm are {Enter} and {Don't Enter}. But there are two decision nodes for the incumbent firm, one decision node is at which the new firm chooses {Don't Enter} and in this case the incumbent firm does not need to make a choice. At the other decision node the new firm chooses {Enter}, and then the incumbent firm chooses {Price War} or {No Price War}. Because a strategy has to specify a complete list of actions that a player would act under all circumstances, so even the new firm chooses {Don't Enter}, the incumbent firm has to plan what it would do if the new firm suddenly chooses {Enter}. For this reason, the incumbent firm has to plan to choose {Price War} or {No Price War} in the case the new firm chooses {Don't Enter}. Therefore, in this game there are four pairs of strategies, namely, (Don't Enter, No Price War), (Don't Enter, Price War), (Enter, No Price War), and (Enter, Price War). Since the game is well defined, we can first use normal form representation to describe the game as depicted in Table 9.1. It turns out that there are two Nash Equilibria for this game: (Don't Enter, Price War) and (Enter, No Price War).

Table 9.1

		Incumbent Firm	
		No Price War	Price War
New Firm	Don't Enter	0, <u>10</u>	<u>0</u>, <u>10</u>
	Enter	<u>4</u>, <u>4</u>	-6, 2

Given that there are two possible equilibrium outcomes in this game, the prediction of the outcome of the game becomes less accurate and precise. Thus, in order to refine the equilibrium outcomes, we have to eliminate an outcome that is not sensible from the point of view of economics.

9.1 Subgame Perfect Equilibrium

We now analyze two Nash equilibrium outcomes to see which one is more reasonable. Let's consider (Don't Enter, Price War} first. For this pair of strategies, the new firm is threatened not to enter the market because if she enters the market the incumbent firm will declare a price war. Is this threat credible? Is it reliable that if the new firm enters the market and then the incumbent firm will declare a price war? This is not really the case, because the incumbent has no commitment or incentive to do so. Let's look at Figure 9.2, if the new firms enters the market then the incumbent firm has two strategies, i.e. {Price War} and {No Price War}. From the perspective of the incumbent firm, the payoff of choosing {No Price War} is 4 but that of choosing {Price War} is 2. So, it is obvious that if the new firm actually enters the market, the incumbent firm will not declare a price war. So, the threat of declaring a price war is not credible. The Nash Equilibrium (Enter, Price War) is not feasible on economic grounds.

There are two subgames in the case of price war. One is the game itself and the other is at the decision node of the incumbent firm. We now define **Subgame Perfect Equilbrium** as Nash Equilbrium in all subgames. As discussed before, we find that if the subgame started at the decision node of the incumbent firm, the optimal decision is to choose {No Price War}. Hence, (Enter, Price War) cannot constitute a Nash Equilibrium in this subgame and thus is not a Subgame Perfect Equilibrium.

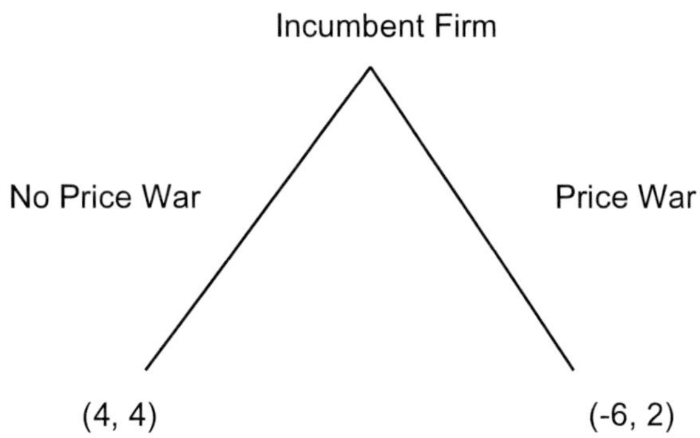

Figure 9.2

Backward Induction

A Subgame Perfect Equilibrium is easily found by using backward induction. In this case the game is solved from the terminal decision node and worked backwards to the initial decision node. At each decision node we have to find the optimal choice for the corresponding player. For this reason, the pair of strategies is optimal in every subgame. In our example, we have to think from the perspective of the incumbent firm, she has to choose {Price War} or {No Price War}. By weighing the payoffs between these two strategies, she will choose {No Price War}. Next, we have to think from the perspective of the new firm. Given that the new firm knows the payoff of each strategy of the incumbent firm, if the new firm thinks that the incumbent firm will act rationally, then the new firm could make a decision conditioned that the incumbent firm chooses {No Price War}. Hence, the new firm has to think about when she enters the market she could get \$4 profit if the incumbent rationally chooses {No Price War}, and when she gets zero if she does not enter the market. So, it is obvious that the new firm will choose {Enter}. Therefore, the Subgame Perfect Equilibrium is (Enter, No Price War) and is depicted in Figure 9.3.

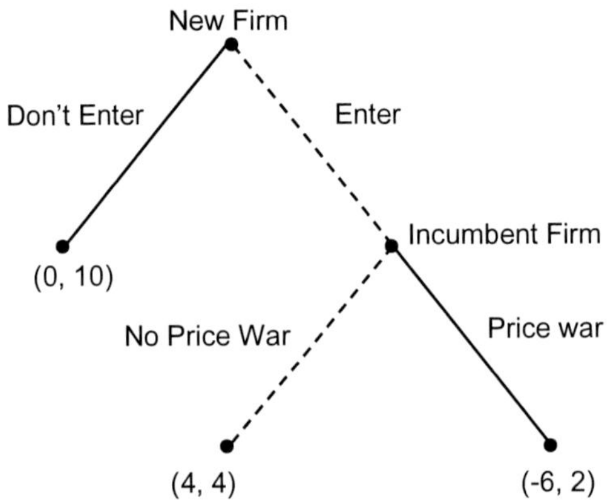

Figure 9.3

STACKELBERG GAME

In Chapter 8 we presented the Cournot game in which the output levels of two firms are simultaneously determined. Now we proceed to analyze a game in which firm 1 is a leader in choosing its quantity of output and firm 2 observe firm 1's quantity and then choose its quantity of output. Such interactive situation fits into the analysis of sequential games. The basic setup is the same as Cournot game as the aggregate output is denoted by $Y = y_1 + y_2$ and the aggregate inverse demand by $p = a - bY$. The cost functions of the firm leader (firm 1) and firm follower (firm 2) are $c_1(y_1) = cy_1$ and $c_2(y_2) = cy_2$, where $c < a$.

We apply the backward induction to solve the equilibrium outcome of this game. Hence, the firm follower's profit maximization problem is:

$$\max_{y_2} \pi_2(y_1, y_2) = [a - b(y_1 + y_2)]y_2 - cy_2$$

The first order condition is $\frac{\partial \pi_2(y_1, y_2)}{\partial y_2} = a - c - 2by_2 - by_1 = 0$ and $y_2 = \frac{a - c - by_1}{2b}$.

The firm leader takes into account what output level would the firm follower produce when determining its own output, so $y_2 = \frac{a - c - by_1}{2b}$ is inserted into the profit maximization problem of the firm leader. We have:

$$\max_{y_1} \pi_1(y_1, y_2) - \left[u - b\left(y_1 + \frac{a - c - by_1}{2b}\right)\right] y_1 - cy_1$$

The first order condition is $\frac{\partial \pi_1(y_1, y_2)}{\partial y_1} = \frac{a - c}{2} - by_1 = 0$

The optimal output of the firm leader is computed as $y_1^* = \frac{a - c}{2b}$. By plugging $y_1^* = \frac{a - c}{2b}$ into $y_2 = \frac{a - c - by_1}{2b}$, we can find the optimal output of the firm follower is $y_2^* = \frac{a - c}{4b}$. So, there is a first-mover advantage in the Stackelberg Game as $y_1^* > y_2^*$.

Chapter 10

MATHEMATICS FOR MICROECONOMICS

In this chapter we will briefly revise matrix algebra, multivariate calculus, and optimization theory to help the reader understand the core microeconomics presented in these lecture notes.

MATRIX ALGEBRA

Matrix Operation

A matrix *A* of size $m \times n$ is an array with *m* rows and *n* columns of real numbers given by

$A = \begin{bmatrix} a_{11} & \cdots & a_{1n} \\ \vdots & \ddots & \vdots \\ a_{m1} & \cdots & a_{mn} \end{bmatrix}$. The *i*th row of *A* is $\begin{bmatrix} a_{i1} & a_{i2} & \ldots & a_{in} \end{bmatrix}$ and *j*th column of *A* is $\begin{bmatrix} a_{1j} \\ a_{2j} \\ \vdots \\ a_{mj} \end{bmatrix}$. The transpose of an $m \times n$ matrix *A* is the $n \times m$ matrix A^T obtained by interchanging the rows and columns of *A*. So, $A^T = \begin{bmatrix} a_{11} & \cdots & a_{m1} \\ \vdots & \ddots & \vdots \\ a_{1n} & \cdots & a_{mn} \end{bmatrix}$. The product of a scalar α and a matrix *A* is $\alpha A = \begin{bmatrix} \alpha a_{11} & \cdots & \alpha a_{1n} \\ \vdots & \ddots & \vdots \\ \alpha a_{m1} & \cdots & \alpha a_{mn} \end{bmatrix}$. Let *B* be a matrix of size $m \times n$, then the sum of A and B is $A+B=\begin{bmatrix} a_{11}+b_{11} & \cdots & a_{1n}+b_{1n} \\ \vdots & \ddots & \vdots \\ a_{m1}+b_{m1} & \cdots & a_{mn}+b_{mn} \end{bmatrix}$. The product of matrix $A \cdot X = Y$ is defined if the number of columns of in A is equal to the number of rows in X. If A is $m \times p$ and X is $p \times n$, then Y will be $m \times n$ matrix, which has its (i, j) element, given by $y_{ij} = (A)_i (X)_j = \sum_{k=1}^{p} a_{ik} x_{kj}$. For example, suppose $A = \begin{bmatrix} 2 & 0 \\ 1 & 4 \\ 3 & 1 \end{bmatrix}$ and $X = \begin{bmatrix} 2 \\ 3 \end{bmatrix}$, then $Y = A \cdot X$ is the (3×1) matrix given by $Y = \begin{bmatrix} 4 \\ 14 \\ 9 \end{bmatrix}$. Finally, a square matrix is defined as one in which the number of rows is equal to the number of columns in the matrix.

The Cramer's Rule

The determinant of A denoted by $|A|$, exists only if A is a square matrix. Let A be a 1×1 matrix $A = [a]$, then $|A| = a$. Let A be a 2×2 matrix $A = \begin{bmatrix} a & b \\ c & d \end{bmatrix}$, then $|A| = ad - bc$. Let A be a 3×3 matrix $A = \begin{bmatrix} a_{11} & a_{12} & a_{13} \\ a_{21} & a_{22} & a_{23} \\ a_{31} & a_{32} & a_{33} \end{bmatrix}$, then

$$|A| = a_{11} \begin{bmatrix} a_{22} & a_{23} \\ a_{32} & a_{33} \end{bmatrix} - a_{12} \begin{bmatrix} a_{21} & a_{23} \\ a_{31} & a_{33} \end{bmatrix} + a_{13} \begin{bmatrix} a_{21} & a_{22} \\ a_{31} & a_{32} \end{bmatrix}.$$

Suppose we have the following system of linear equations

$$\begin{aligned} a_{11}x_1 + a_{12}x_2 + a_{13}x_3 &= y_1 \\ a_{21}x_1 + a_{22}x_2 + a_{23}x_3 &= y_2 \\ a_{31}x_1 + a_{32}x_2 + a_{33}x_3 &= y_3 \end{aligned}$$

It can be written as $A \cdot X = Y$, where

$A = \begin{bmatrix} a_{11} & a_{12} & a_{13} \\ a_{21} & a_{22} & a_{23} \\ a_{31} & a_{32} & a_{33} \end{bmatrix}$, $X = \begin{bmatrix} x_1 \\ x_2 \\ x_3 \end{bmatrix}$, and $Y = \begin{bmatrix} y_1 \\ y_2 \\ y_3 \end{bmatrix}$. Given that $|A| \neq 0$, we can find the value of $X = \begin{bmatrix} x_1 \\ x_2 \\ x_3 \end{bmatrix}$ by using the Cramer's Rule:

$$x_1 = \frac{\begin{vmatrix} y_1 & a_{12} & a_{13} \\ y_2 & a_{22} & a_{23} \\ y_3 & a_{32} & a_{33} \end{vmatrix}}{|A|}, \; x_2 = \frac{\begin{vmatrix} a_{11} & y_1 & a_{13} \\ a_{21} & y_2 & a_{23} \\ a_{31} & y_3 & a_{33} \end{vmatrix}}{|A|}, \text{ and } x_3 = \frac{\begin{vmatrix} a_{11} & a_{12} & y_1 \\ a_{21} & a_{22} & y_2 \\ a_{31} & a_{32} & y_3 \end{vmatrix}}{|A|}.$$

Cramer's Rule allows us to solve for each x_i. The procedure is to replace the *i*th column of *A* by *Y*, and then we compute the determinant of this new matrix. Finally, x_i is computed by dividing the determinant of this new matrix by the determinant of *A*, where $|A| \neq 0$.

For example, we have a system of linear equation

$$\begin{aligned} 2x_1 + x_2 - 3x_3 &= 10 \\ x_1 + x_2 - x_3 &= 5 \\ 3x_1 + 4x_2 + 5x_3 &= 1 \end{aligned}, \text{ where } A = \begin{bmatrix} 2 & 1 & -3 \\ 1 & 1 & -1 \\ 3 & 4 & 5 \end{bmatrix}, \; x = \begin{bmatrix} x_1 \\ x_2 \\ x_3 \end{bmatrix}, \text{ and } y = \begin{bmatrix} 10 \\ 5 \\ 1 \end{bmatrix}.$$ Given that

$|A| = 7$, so by the Cramer's Rule,

$$x_1 = \frac{\begin{vmatrix} 10 & 1 & -3 \\ 5 & 1 & -1 \\ 1 & 4 & 5 \end{vmatrix}}{|A|} = 1, \; x_2 = \frac{\begin{vmatrix} 2 & 10 & -3 \\ 1 & 5 & -1 \\ 3 & 1 & 5 \end{vmatrix}}{|A|} = 2, \text{ and } x_3 = \frac{\begin{vmatrix} 2 & 1 & 10 \\ 1 & 1 & 5 \\ 3 & 4 & 1 \end{vmatrix}}{|A|} = -2.$$

MULTIVARIATE CALCULUS

Partial Differentiation

Suppose we have a function $y = f(x, z)$, where *y* is a function of variables *x* and *z*. We are interested in examining the slope between *y* and *x* or the rate of change in *y* per unit change in *x*, assuming that *z* is constant. In calculus, this is equivalent to partially differentiating *y* with respect to *x*. It means that differentiating *y* with respect to *x*, holding other variables being constant. This is written as $\frac{\partial y}{\partial x} = f_x(x, z)$. If $f_x(x, z) > 0$, an increase in *x* causes *y* to increase; if $f_x(x, z) < 0$, an increase in *x* causes *y* to decrease. If we want to know the rate at which this slope is changing, we can differentiate $f_x(x, z)$ with respect to *x* again, so $\frac{\partial^2 y}{\partial x^2} = f_{xx}(x, z)$. If $f_{xx}(x, z) > 0$, the rate of change of this slope is increasing; if $f_{xx}(x, z) < 0$, the rate of change of this slope is decreasing. If we want to know how an increase in *z* cause $f_x(x, z)$ to change, we can differentiate $f_x(x, z)$ with respect to *z*, namely, $\frac{\partial^2 y}{\partial z \partial x} = f_{xz}(x,z)$. By the Young Theorem, $f_{xz}(x,z) = f_{zx}(x,z)$, which implies that the order of cross partial differentiation does not matter.

For a concrete example, let $y = f(k,h) = Ak^{\alpha}h^{\beta}$, given $A > 0$, $0 < \alpha < 1$, and $0 < \beta < 1$. We have:

$$\frac{\partial y}{\partial k} = \frac{\partial\left(Ak^{\alpha}h^{\beta}\right)}{\partial k} = \alpha Ak^{\alpha-1}h^{\beta} > 0$$

$$\frac{\partial^2 y}{\partial k^2} = \frac{\partial\left(\alpha Ak^{\alpha-1}h^{\beta}\right)}{\partial k} = \alpha(\alpha-1)Ak^{\alpha-2}h^{\beta} < 0$$

$$\frac{\partial y}{\partial h} = \frac{\partial\left(Ak^{\alpha}h^{\beta}\right)}{\partial h} = \beta Ak^{\alpha}h^{\beta-1} > 0$$

$$\frac{\partial^2 y}{\partial h^2} = \frac{\partial\left(\beta Ak^{\alpha}h^{\beta-1}\right)}{\partial h} = \beta(\beta-1)Akh^{\beta-2} < 0$$

$$\frac{\partial^2 y}{\partial h \partial k} = \frac{\partial\left(\alpha Ak^{\alpha-1}h^{\beta}\right)}{\partial h} = \alpha\beta Ak^{\alpha-1}h^{\beta-1} = \frac{\partial\left(\beta Ak^{\alpha}h^{\beta-1}\right)}{\partial k} = \frac{\partial^2 y}{\partial k \partial h} > 0,$$ which confirms the Young Theorem.

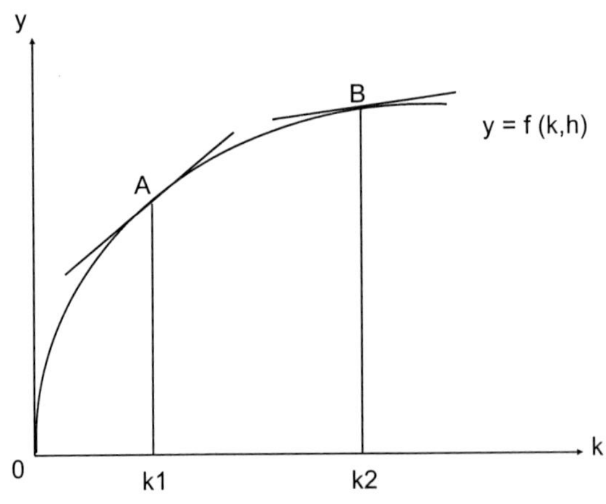

Figure 10.1

Figure 10.1 illustrate a two-dimensional graph between *y* and *k*, where *y* is the dependent variable and *k* is the independent variable, given that $\overline{h}$ is constant. Point *A* is the slope between y and k when $k = k_1$, namely, $\left.\frac{\partial y}{\partial k}\right|_{k=k_1} = \alpha k_1^{\alpha-1}\overline{h}^{\beta} > 0$. It also shows that the slope becomes smaller as k increases, say, from k_1 to k_2. So, $\frac{\partial^2 y}{\partial k^2} = \alpha(\alpha-1)k_1^{\alpha-2}\overline{h}^{\beta} < 0$. The intuition behind this result is the value of y is positive when we increase one unit of k, but the rate of an increase of y diminishes as k increases. Moreover, y is a concave function of k, or y is concave in k. See text for a more rigorous definition of a concave function.

Implicit Function and Total Differentiation

Previously, we define y as an explicit function of k and h given by $y = f(k,h) = Ak^{\alpha}h^{\beta}$. Alternatively, we can rewrite it as an implicit function $g(k,h,y) = 0$. We totally differentiate $g(k,h,y) = 0$, then $\frac{\partial g(k,h,y)}{\partial k}dk + \frac{\partial g(k,h,y)}{\partial h}dh + \frac{\partial g(k,h,y)}{\partial y}dy = 0$. Given y is constant, $\frac{\partial g(k,h,y)}{\partial y}dy = 0$, and so we have $\frac{dh}{dk} = -\frac{\partial g(k,h,y)/\partial k}{\partial g(k,h,y)/\partial h}$. Figure 10.2 depicts the case of $y = f(k,h) = Ak^{\alpha}h^{\beta}$. The horizontal axis measures the quantity of k and the vertical axis measures the quantity of h. It is a contour between k and h given a fixed value of y. Point A is a slope between k and h and is given by $\frac{dh}{dk} = -\frac{\alpha Ak^{\alpha-1}h^{\beta}}{\beta Ak^{\alpha}h^{\beta-1}} = -\frac{\alpha h}{\beta k} < 0$, holding y is constant. We find that the slope is increasing with an increase in k, i.e. $\frac{d^2h}{dk^2} = \frac{\alpha h}{\beta k^2} > 0$. It is obvious to see that the slope at point B is larger than the slope at point A where k is smaller.

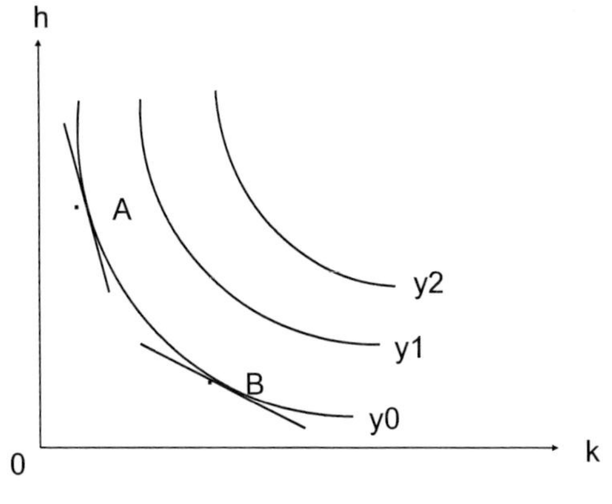

Figure 10.2

Homogeneous Function

Suppose we multiply all the independent variables of $f(x,z)$ by t, then the function is homogenous of degree k if $t^k f(x,z) = f(tx,tz)$. If $k=0$, then the function is homogeneous of degree zero; if $k=1$, then the function is homogeneous of degree one.

For example, $y = Ak^\alpha h^\beta$. We find that $A(tk)^\alpha (th)^\beta = t^{\alpha+\beta} Ak^\alpha h^\beta = t^{\alpha+\beta} f(x,z)$. So, this function is homogeneous of degree $\alpha+\beta$.

Alternatively, according to the Euler's Theorem, $f(x,z)$ is homogeneous of degree k if and only if $kf(x,z) = \frac{\partial f(x,z)}{\partial x}x + \frac{\partial f(x,z)}{\partial z}z$. For simplicity, we use $f(k,h) = Ak^\alpha h^\beta$ as an example to verify this theorem. Since $\frac{\partial\left(Ak^\alpha h^\beta\right)}{\partial k} = \alpha Ak^{\alpha-1}h^\beta$ and $\frac{\partial\left(Ak^\alpha h^\beta\right)}{\partial h} = \beta Ak^\alpha h^{\beta-1}$, so

$$\frac{\partial\left(Ak^\alpha h^\beta\right)}{\partial k}k + \frac{\partial\left(Ak^\alpha h^\beta\right)}{\partial h}h = \alpha Ak^\alpha h^\beta + \beta Ak^\alpha h^\beta = (\alpha+\beta)f(k,h)$$

Therefore, $f(k,h) = Ak^\alpha h^\beta$ is homogeneous of degree $\alpha+\beta$, which is consistent with our previous result.

Constrained Optimization

Suppose we want to maximize $y = f(x,z)$ subject to the constraint $g(x,z) = 0$, that is to find values of x and z such that the constraint is satisfied. We can make use of Lagrangian multiplier method to solve the optimal values x^* and z^*,

Formally, we can write the Lagrangian as:

$$\Omega(x,z,\lambda) = f(x,z) - \lambda g(x,z)$$

The Lagrangian Ω is a function of x, z, and λ. To find the first order conditions, we differentiate Ω with respect to x, z, and λ. It follows that:

$$\frac{\partial\Omega}{\partial\lambda} = -g(x,z) = 0$$

$$\frac{\partial \Omega}{\partial x} = f_x(x,z) - \lambda g_x(x,z) = 0$$

$$\frac{\partial \Omega}{\partial z} = f_z(x,z) - \lambda g_z(x,z) = 0$$

Since there are three equations with three unknowns, we can solve for the optimal values x^*, z^*, and λ^*.

In order to determine whether x^* and z^* are maximized values, we have to check the second order condition. Before doing so, we differentiate equations (1) to (3) with respect to x, z, and λ, respectively. After some algebra, we find the following 3x3 Borderd Hessian matrix:

$$\begin{bmatrix} \frac{\partial^2 \Omega}{\partial \lambda \partial \lambda} & \frac{\partial^2 \Omega}{\partial x \partial \lambda} & \frac{\partial^2 \Omega}{\partial z \partial \lambda} \\ \frac{\partial^2 \Omega}{\partial \lambda \partial x} & \frac{\partial^2 \Omega}{\partial x \partial x} & \frac{\partial^2 \Omega}{\partial z \partial x} \\ \frac{\partial^2 \Omega}{\partial \lambda \partial z} & \frac{\partial^2 \Omega}{\partial x \partial z} & \frac{\partial^2 \Omega}{\partial z \partial \lambda} \end{bmatrix} = \begin{bmatrix} 0 & -g_x(x,z) & -g_z(x,z) \\ -g_x(x,z) & f_{xx}(x,z) - \lambda g_{xx}(x,z) & f_{xz}(x,z) - \lambda g_{xz}(x,z) \\ -g_z(x,z) & f_{zx}(x,z) - \lambda g_{zx}(x,z) & f_{zz}(x,z) - \lambda g_{zz}(x,z) \end{bmatrix}$$

For a maximum, it requires the 3x3 bordered Hessian to be:

$$\begin{vmatrix} 0 & -g_{xx}(x,z) & -g_{zz}(x,z) \\ -g_x(x,z) & f_{xx}(x,z) - \lambda g_{xx}(x,z) & f_{xz}(x,z) - \lambda g_{xz}(x,z) \\ -g_z(x,z) & f_{zx}(x,z) - \lambda g_{zx}(x,z) & f_{zz}(x,z) - \lambda g_{zz}(x,z) \end{vmatrix} > 0.$$

For a minimum, it requires the 3x3 bordered Hessian to be:

$$\begin{vmatrix} 0 & -g_{xx}(x,z) & -g_{zz}(x,z) \\ -g_x(x,z) & f_{xx}(x,z) - \lambda g_{xx}(x,z) & f_{xz}(x,z) - \lambda g_{xz}(x,z) \\ -g_z(x,z) & f_{zx}(x,z) - \lambda g_{zx}(x,z) & f_{zz}(x,z) - \lambda g_{zz}(x,z) \end{vmatrix} < 0.$$

We provide the following numerical example:

Suppose we have to maximize $U = x^{0.3} z^{0.7}$ subject to $2x + 5z = 100$. First, we form the Lagrangian as:

$$\Omega(x,z,\lambda) = x^{0.3} z^{0.7} - \lambda(2x + 5z - 100)$$

We differentiate Ω with respect to λ, x, and z. It follows that:

$$\frac{\partial\Omega}{\partial\lambda} = 100 - 2x - 5z = 0$$

$$\frac{\partial\Omega}{\partial x} = \frac{3}{10}\left(\frac{z}{x}\right)^{0.7} - 2\lambda = 0$$

$$\frac{\partial\Omega}{\partial z} = \frac{7}{10}\left(\frac{x}{z}\right)^{0.3} - 5\lambda = 0$$

After some simple algebra, we find $x^* = 15$ and $z^* = 14$. In order to know these values of x and z are maximized value, we have to check the second order condition: We differentiate respectively three first order conditions with respect to λ, x, and z to get the following Bordered Hessian matrix:

$$\begin{bmatrix} \frac{\partial^2\Omega}{\partial\lambda\partial\lambda} & \frac{\partial^2\Omega}{\partial x\partial\lambda} & \frac{\partial^2\Omega}{\partial z\partial\lambda} \\ \frac{\partial^2\Omega}{\partial\lambda\partial x} & \frac{\partial^2\Omega}{\partial x\partial x} & \frac{\partial^2\Omega}{\partial z\partial x} \\ \frac{\partial^2\Omega}{\partial\lambda\partial z} & \frac{\partial^2\Omega}{\partial x\partial z} & \frac{\partial^2\Omega}{\partial z\partial\lambda} \end{bmatrix} = \begin{bmatrix} 0 & -2 & -5 \\ -2 & -0.21x^{-1.7}z^{0.7} & 0.21x^{-0.7}z^{-0.3} \\ -5 & 0.21x^{-0.7}z^{-0.3} & -0.21x^{0.3}z^{-1.3} \end{bmatrix}$$

We find that:

$$\begin{vmatrix} 0 & -2 & -5 \\ -2 & -0.21x^{-1.7}z^{0.7} & 0.21x^{-0.7}z^{-0.3} \\ -5 & 0.21x^{-0.7}z^{-0.3} & -0.21x^{-1.7}z^{0.7} \end{vmatrix} = 2\begin{vmatrix} -2 & 0.21x^{-0.7}z^{-0.3} \\ -5 & -0.21x^{0.3}z^{-1.3} \end{vmatrix} - 5\begin{vmatrix} -2 & -0.21x^{-1.7}z^{0.7} \\ -5 & 0.21x^{-0.7}z^{-0.3} \end{vmatrix} > 0$$

Therefore, $x^* = 15$ and $z^* = 14$ are the maximized values of this constrained maximization problem.

Envelope Theorem

Suppose we want to maximize a value function $U = x \cdot z$ subjective to a constraint $p_x x + p_z z = y$, where x and z are functions of parameters p_x, p_z, and y. We can write the Lagrangian as:

$\Omega = U\left(x(p_x, p_z, y)\cdot z(p_x, p_z, y)\right) - \lambda\left(p_x x(p_x, p_z, y) + p_z z(p_x, p_z, y) - y\right)$. By the Envelope Theorem, the effect of an increase in one of parameters, for example, p_x, on the value function is:

$\dfrac{\partial U\left(p_x, p_z, y\right)}{\partial p_x} = \dfrac{\partial \Omega}{\partial p_x} = -\lambda x$, where λ and x are the optimized values satisfying the constraint.

REFERENCES

[1] Afriat, S.A. (1966). Economic Transformation. *Krannert Institute, Paper No. 152, Purdue University, Nov. 1966.*

[2] Afriat, S. (1967). The construction of utility functions from expenditure data. *International Economic Review,* 8:67-77.

[3] Alchian, A. (1953). The Meaning of Utility Measurement. *American Economic Review, vol. 43 (Mar 1953)*, 26-50. Reprinted in W. Breit and H.M. Hochman (Ed.), *Readings in Microeconomics*: (chapter 5, pp. 69-88).

[4] Allen, R.G.D. (1938). *Mathematical Analysis for Economists*, London: Macmillan.

[5] Arrow, K.J. (1950). An Extension of the Basic Theorems of Classical Welfare Economics. In J. Neyman (1950) (Ed.), *Proceedings of the Second Berkeley Symposium on Mathematical Statistics and Probability* (pp. 507-32). Reprinted in P. Newman (ed.) (1968). *Readings in Mathematical Economics* (*vol. 1).*

[6] Arrow, K.J. (1951). *Social Choice and Individual Values* (2nd ed. 1963). Yale University Press.

[7] Arrow, K.J. (1964). *Aspects of the Theory of Risk-Bearing.* Helsinki: The Academic Book Store, 1965.

[8] Arrow, K.J. (1968). Economic Equilibrium. *International Encyclopedia of the Social Sciences*, *vol. 4,* 376-86. Macmillan Co. of New York and The Free Press.

[9] Arrow, K.J. and F.H. Hahn (1971), *General Competitive Analysis.* Edinburgh, Oliver & Boyd.

[10] Barten, A.P. (1964). Consumer Demand Functions Under Conditions of Almost Additive Preferences . *Econometrica, vol. 32,* 1-38.

[11] Becker, G.S. (1962). Irrational Behaviour and Economic Theory. *Journal of Political Economy, vol. 70,* 1-13.

[12] Bhagwati, J. The Generalized Theory of Distortions and Welfare.

[13] Brown, A. and A. Deaton (1972). Models of Consumer Behaviour: A Survey. *Economic Journal, vol. 82,* 1145-1236.

[14] Chipman, J.S., et al (1971). *Preferences, Utility and Demand.* A Minnesota Symposium. New York, Harcourt Brace Jovanovich Inc.

[15] Chipman, J.S. (1971). Consumption Theory without Transitive Preferences. In L.J.S. Chipman et al. (1971) (Ed.), *Preferences, Utility and Demand:* (*chapter 11*). New York: Harcourt Brace Jovanovich Inc.

[16] Courant, R., and H. Robbins (1941). *What is Mathematics?* Oxford University Press.

[17] Deaton, A., and Muellbauer, J. (1980). *Economics and Consumer Behaviour.* Cambridge.U.K: Cambridge University Press.

[18] Debreu, G. (1959). Topological Methods in Cardinal Utility Theory. In K.J. Arrow et al., *Mathematical Methods in the Social Sciences 1959.* Stanford University Press.

[19] Debreu, G. (1954). Representation of a Preference Ordering by a Numerical Function. In R. Thrall, C. Coombs, and R. Davis (Ed.), *Decision Processes.* New York: John Wiley and Sons.

[20] Debreu, G. (1959). *Theory of Value: An Axiomatic Analysis of Economic Equilibrium.* Yale University Press.

[21] Debreu, G. (1960). Topological Methods in Cardinal Utility. In K. Arrow, S. Karlin, and P. Suppes (Ed.), *Mathematical Methods in the Social Studies 1959.* Stanford, Calif.: Stanford University Press.

[22] Diewert, W.E. (1982). Duality Approaches to Microeconomic Theory. In K. Arrow and M. Intriligator (Ed.), *Handbook of Mathematical Economics* (*Vol. 2, Chapter 12*). Amsterdam: North Holland.

[23] Dorfman, R.,P. Samuelson and R. Solow (1958). *Linear Programming Analysis*. New York: McGraw-Hill.

[24] Duesenberry, J. S. (1949). *Income, Saving and the Theory of Consumer Behaviour.* New York, Galaxy Book, Oxford University Press 1967. Originally published by Cambridge, U.S.A: Harvard University Press,.

[25] Edgeworth, F. Y. (1881). *Mathematical Psychics.* London: Kegan Paul.

[26] Ellsburg, D. (1954). Classical and Current Notions of Measurable Utility. *Economic Journal, vol. 64,* 528-556. Reprinted in A. N. Page (1968) (Ed.), *Utility Theory: A Book of Readings.* London: John Wiley.

[27] Fishburn, P. (1970) 1979. *Utility Theory for Decision Making.* New York: John Wiley and Sons. Reprinted in Huntington, N.Y.: R. E. Krieger Publishing.

[28] Friedman, M. (1953). *Essays in Positive Economics.* Chicago: University of Chicago press, Phoenix ed. 1966.

[29] Gale, D. (1960). *Theory of Linear Economic Models.* New York: McGraw-Hill.

[30] Gibbons, R. (1992). *A Primer in Game Theory.* New York : Harvester Wheatsheaf.

[31] Graaff, J. de V. (1957). *Theoretical Welfare Economics.* Cambridge University Press.

[32] Green, J.R. and Heller, W. (1981). Mathematical Analysis and Convexity With Application to Economics. In K. Arrow and M. Intriligator. Amsterdam, North Holland (Ed.), *Handbook of Mathematical Economics* (*Vol. 1. Chapter 1*).

[33] Hicks, J. R. (1939). *Value and Capital.* Oxford: Clarendon Press.

[34] Hicks, J. R. (1939) Value and Capital (2nd edition. 1946). Oxford University Press.

[35] Hicks, J. R. and R. G. D. Allen (1934). A Reconsideration of the Theory of Value. *Economica, vol. 1,* 52-76 and 196-219.

[36] Houthakker, H. S. (1950). Revealed Preferences and the Utility Function. *Economica, vol. 17,* 159-174.

[37] Houthakker, H. S. (1960). Additive Preferences. *Econometrica, vol. 28,* 244-257. Reprinted in A. Zellner (1968) (Ed.), *Readings in Economic Statistics and Econometrics.* Boston, Little, Brown & Co.

[38] Jehle, G. A., and P. J. Reny (2001). *Advanced Microeconomic Theory.* Boston : Addison-Wesley

[39] Jorgenson, D. W. (1960). A dual Stability Theorem. *Econometrica, vol. 28,* 892-9.

[40] Kakutani, S. (1941). A Generalization of Brouwer's Fixed-Point Theorem. *Duke Mathematical Journal, vol. 9,* 457-459. Reprinted in P. Newman (1968) (Ed.), *Readings in Mathematical Economics* (*vol. I. Value Theory*). Baltimore: Johns Hopkins Press.

[41] Kannai, Y. (1977). Concavifiability and Constructions of Concave utility Functions. *Journal of Mathematical Economics 4*:1-56.

[42] Katzner, D. (1970). *Static Demand Theory.* New York: Macmillan. Varian, H. (1984). *Microeconomic Analysis* (2nd edition). New York: W. W. Norton.

[43] Koopmans, T. C. (1957). *Three Essays on the State of Economic Science*. London: McGraw-Hill.
[44] Kreps, D.M. (1992). *A Course in Microeconomic Theory.* New Delhi Prentice-Hall of India.
[45] Laffont, J. J. (1989). *Fundamentals of Public Economics.* MIT Press: Cambridge Mass.
[46] Leontief, W. (1937). Implicit Theorizing: A Methodological Criticism of the Neo-Cambridge School. *Quarterly Journal of Economics, vol. 51,* 337-51. Also in W. Leontief (1966). *Essays in Economics: Theories and Theorizing.* Oxford University Press.
[47] Leontief, W. (1966). *Essays in Economics: Theories and Theorizing.* Oxford University Press.
[48] Lipsey, R. G., and K. Lancaster (1956-1957).The General Theory of thc Second Best. *Review of Economic Studies, vol. 24,* 11-32.
[49] Luce, R. D. (1959). *Individual Choice Behaviour: A Theoretical Analysis*. New York: Wiley.
[50] Mas-Colell, A., Whiston, M. D., and G. Green (1995). *Microeconomic Theory*. New York : Oxford University Press.
[51] McKenzie, L. (1960). Matrices with Dominant Diagonals and Economic Theory. In K. J. Arrow et al. (Ed.), *Mathematical Methods in the Social Sciences, 1959.* California: Stanford University.
[52] Nikaido, H. (1968). *Convex Structures and Economic Theory: vol. 51.* London: Academic Press.
[53] Richter, M. K. (1971). Rational Choice. In J. S. Chipman et al. (1971) (Ed.), *Preferences, Utility and Demand.* New York: Harcourt Brace Jovanovich Inc.
[54] Robbins, L. (1932). *An Essay on the Nature and Significance of Economic Science,* (2nd edition. 1935). London: Macmillan.
[55] Samuelson, P. A. (1947). *Foundations of Economic Analysis*. Harvard University Press. Harvard Economic Studies, LXXX.
[56] Samuelson, P. (1947). *Foundations of Economic Analysis*. Cambridge, Mass.: Harvard University Press.
[57] Shapley, L. S. and M. Shubik (1967). Concepts and Theories and Pure Competition. In M. Shubik (Ed.), *Essays in Mathematical Economics. Essays in Honor of Oskar Morgenstern.* Princeton University Press.
[58] Slutsky, E. E. (1915). On the Theory of the Budget of the Consumer. *Giornale degli Economisti: vol. LI,* 1-26. Reprinted in *Readings in Price Theory*: ch. 2, 27-56.
[59] Slutsky, E. (1915). Sulla teoria del bilancio del consumatore. *Giernali degle Economisti 51,* 1-26. (English translation: on the theory of the budget of the consumer, In G. Stigles and K. Boulding (Ed.), *Readings in Price Theory*. Chicago: Richard Irwin, 1952.
[60] Sonnenschein, H. F. (1971). Demand Theory without Transitive Preferences. With Applications to the Theory of Competitive Equilibrium. In J. S. Chipman et al. (Ed.), *Preferences, Utility and Demand: ch. 10.* New York: Harcourt Brace Jovanovich Inc.
[61] Starrett, D. (1972). Fundamental Non-convexities in the Theory of Externalities. *Journal of Economic Theory, 4,* 180-199.
[62] Varian, H. (1984). *Microeconomic Analysis (2nd edition)*. New York: Norton.
[63] Varian, H. (1992). *Microeconomic Analysis (Third Edition)*. New York: Norton.
[64] Whitaker, J. K., and B. T. McCallum (1971). On Homotheticity of Production Functions. *Western Economic Journal, vol. 9,* 57-63.

INDEX

A

B

C